To Fu ...

1947 ...

D1029901

"JUST CALIFORNIA" AND OTHER POEMS

JOHN STEVEN McGROARTY

1933
The TIMES-MIRROR *Press*
LOS ANGELES

"*I have washed my hands in the winds,*
I have cleansed my mouth in the rain,
I have put on my robe of roses.
And the crown of my little songs."

CONTENTS

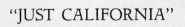

"JUST CALIFORNIA"

"JUST CALIFORNIA"

When I am in California I am not in the West.
It is West of the West. It is just California.
                              —Theodore Roosevelt

'Twixt the seas and the deserts,
    'Twixt the wastes and the waves,
Between the sands of buried lands
    And ocean's coral caves;
It lies not East nor West,
    But like a scroll unfurled,
Where the hand of God hath flung it
    Down the middle of the world.

It lies where God hath spread it
    In the gladness of His eyes,
Like a flame of jeweled tapestry
    Beneath His shining skies;
With the green of woven meadows,
    The hills in golden chains,
The light of leaping rivers,
    And the flash of poppied plains.

1

Days rise that gleam in glory,
    Days die with sunset's breeze,
While from Cathay that was of old
    Sail countless argosies;
Morns break again in splendor
    O'er the giant, new-born West,
But of all the lands God fashioned,
    'Tis this land is the best.

Sun and dews that kiss it,
    Balmy winds that blow,
The stars in clustered diadems
    Upon its peaks of snow;
The mighty mountains o'er it,
    Below, the white seas swirled—
Just California, stretching down
    The middle of the world.

THE KING'S HIGHWAY

[*El Camino Real*]

All in the golden weather forth let us ride today,
You and I together on the King's Highway,
The blue skies above us, and below the shining sea;
There's many a road to travel, but it's this road
    for me.

It's a long road and sunny and the fairest in the
    world—
There are peaks that rise above it in their snowy
    mantles curled,
And it leads from the mountains through a hedge
    of chaparral
Down to the waters where the sea-gulls call.

It's a long road and sunny, 'tis a long road and old,
And the brown Padres made it for the flocks of the
    fold;
They made it for the sandals of the sinner-folk that
    trod
From the fields in the open to the shelter-house of
    God.

They made it for the sandals of the sinner-folk of old;
Now the flocks they are scattered and death keeps
  the fold;
But you and I together we will take the road today
With the breath in our nostrils on the King's High-
  way.

We will take the road together through the morn-
  ing's golden glow,
And we'll dream of those who trod it in the mel-
  lowed long ago;
We will stop at the Missions where the sleeping
  Padres lay,
And bend a knee above them for their souls' sake
  to pray.

We'll ride through the valleys where the blossom's
  on the tree,
Through the orchards and the meadows with the
  bird and the bee,
And we'll take the rising hills where the manzanitas
  grow,
Past the gray tails of waterfalls where blue violets
  blow.

Old Conquistadores, O brown priests and all,
Give us your ghosts for company when night begins
    to fall;
There's many a road to travel, but it's this road today,
With the breath of God about us on the King's
    Highway.

LENA OF MUSCOVY

During the Russo-Japanese war, the little Russian gunboat "Lena" put into the harbor of San Francisco and placed itself under the protection of the United States.

In to the sun-kissed harbor,
    In through the Golden Gate,
Under the mouths of the silent guns
    Where the brown hills watch and wait,
Like a hunted thing to the haven,
    Like a wounded gull from sea,
Asking a shelter for old time's sake
    Sailed Lena of Muscovy.

From decks in the fog-wrapped waters,
    From folded sails on the mast,
The sailors saw the dim cliffs rise
    With their memories of the past;
From the foam-swept bow they saw them
    In the mists of the morning cold,
And they saw the gleam of the starry flag
    They knew and loved of old.

6

The brown hills closed around them,
  The waves of the bay sang low,
And the flag flung out its welcome
  To the friends of the long ago.
And though from the fortress leaning
  The shore guns stirred nor spake,
In their iron throats their voices longed
  To shout for "the old sake's sake."

Welcome, brave hearts that loved us,
  Whose strong swords failed us not
When the traitor struck in the darkness
  And the envying world forgot—
White ship from the tumbling ocean,
  Lone wanderer from the sea,
Fold your sails in the friendly port,
  O Lena of Muscovy.

THE CAPTIVE COYOTES

The gray thief's outcast brood,
    Trapped in the haunts of men—
And far away the sheltered wood,
    And far the desert's fen.

Far is the moonlit plain
    Where they would wand'ring be;
They like not through the window pane
    The faces that they see.

No use to stretch a hand
    Of kind and friendly care;
They would not know or understand
    The peace ye would declare.

The wild blood will not tame
    With one day's passing grace;
For, know ye not from whence they came,
    That gaunt, marauding race?

For full a thousand years
    They've borne the bane and ban,
The bold, unshriven buccaneers,
    The gypsy's outlawed clan.

And so, when night stars pale
    And wakes the desert's breeze,
If ye shall hear a she-wolf's wail,
    It is for loss of these.

THE HILLS OF SANTA CRUZ

One time, in Springtime, God made a perfect day,
He woke me in the morning and hid my cares away,
He woke me with the thrush's song, and with the
    linnet's trills;
He took me in His hand and set me on the hills.

He set me on the hills, on the topmost hill of all,
And I heard the morning winds and far sea-breakers
    call,
I heard the winds a-singing from the lands and waters
    met,
And, I live a thousand years, oh, I never can forget.

He touched my eyes with gladness, with balm of
    morning dews,
On the topmost rim He set me 'mong the Hills of
    Santa Cruz.
I saw the sunlit ocean sweep, I saw the vale below—
The Vale of Santa Clara in a sea of blossomed snow.

It was Springtime and joy-time, and God had filled
    His loom
With woven plains of poppies and orchards all
    abloom,
With web of gold and purple in the fields and up-
    lands green,
And the white woof of blossoms that stretched away
    between.

The bluest sky that ever shone stretched over me
    that day,
And I could see the ships that rode upon St. Francis
    Bay;
I could see the ships a-sailing with pennants flung
    elate;
I could see them win the harbor and pass the Golden
    Gate.

Up from the valley, with song and laughter, rose
The voice of happy peoples from the blossomed or-
    chard snows,
The Spring's clear soprano from the gleaming, sway-
    ing trees,
And the basso crescendo of the surf-breaking seas.

One time, in Springtime, God made a perfect day,
He woke my soul to see it, and loosed my heart in
    play,
With the lark's song He woke me and the gull's
    distant call,
And He set me on the hills, on the farthest hill of all.

Bright days of pleasure and gray days of pain—
I've had my willing share of both, and so I may
    again;
'Tis not for me to make them, 'tis not for me to
    choose,
But, oh, that day of splendor in the hills of Santa
    Cruz.

IN THE SAN JOAQUIN

I watched the sun sink in the west,
    I watched the sweet day die;
Above the dim Coast Range's crest
    I saw the red clouds lie;
I saw them lying golden deep,
    By lingering sunbeams kissed,
Like isles of Fairyland that sleep
    In seas of amethyst.

Soft, through the amber twilight, stole
    One clear note of the lark,
As fell upon my wondering soul
    The desert's sudden dark;
It fell with trembling fear that broods
    When night steals o'er the plain,
And from the ghostly cottonwoods
    The moody owls complain.

Then, through the long night hours I lay
    In baffled sleep's travail,
And heard the outcast thieves in gray—
    The gaunt coyotes—wail.
With seaward winds that wandering blew,
    I heard the wild geese cry,
I heard their gray wings beating through
    The star dust of the sky.

Spent, through the wakeful gloom, I lay
    With my poor heart's distress,
And walked again the haunted way
    Of life's old loneliness.
The dead, from far graves come, I heard,
    I saw them rise and pass;
They spoke my name when, sighing stirred
    The whispering pampas grass.

Yet, with the last grim, solemn hour,
    Stilled were the voices all,
And then, from poppied fields a-flower,
    Rang out the wild bird's call;
The glad dawn, deep in white mists steeped,
    Breathed on the day's hushed lyre,
And far the dim Sierras leaped
    In living waves of fire.

IN MONTEREY

[*A Memory of Robert Louis Stevenson*]

When long ago he wandered here,
    Heart-hungered, sick and poor,
No roof was bent to shelter him,
    No welcome at the door.

In all the streets of Monterey,
    With sun and shine aflame,
No word was passed that they might know
    The Prince of Dreamers came.

There sped no song to meet him
    From lute or lifted lyre,
When here the Master Singer passed
    To seek his Heart's Desire.

No hand was raised to help him,
    No lips with cheer to greet,
Till worn with fast and weariness
    He fainted at their feet.

15

Then one there was who lifted up
    The fever-tortured head,
And took him to his pitying heart,
    And gave him drink and bread—

Gave him a shelter and a bed,
    Nor asked his name to know—
And of all the men of Monterey
    It is to him I'll go.

It is to this old, kindly man
    That I will go today,
The thanks of all the grateful world
    And my poor thanks to say.

Let from the shores the wild waves break
    In mist and white sprays flung,
Let from the ancient Mission tower
    The Angelus be rung;

Let all the tales they tell be told,
    But just one tale for me—
And 'tis of him who sleeps afar
    Beyond that sun-kissed sea;

Whose dreams I know, whose songs I sing,
    Though dead he lies and still—
"The sailor who is home from sea,
    The hunter from the hill."

THE BAY OF SAN DIEGO

The sunlight of the morning across the far hills
    broke,
From the dawn the veils of mists fell and faded as
    I woke;
The sea was bathed with glory in a sweep of swirl-
    ing fire,
And I wandered with my soul in the Land of Heart's
    Desire.

In the Land of Heart's Desire, in the dreamland of
    my soul,
And my boat was on the shore with its rudder and
    its thole,
With its white sails agleam and the soft winds blow-
    ing free,
And the Bay of San Diego shining blue against the
    sea.

Yonder from the hills blew the blithe breeze of morn,
The scent of the lemon on its breath of lotus borne,
The scent of the lemon from the mesas blowing
    down,
From Chula Vista's mesas to the sun-harbored town.

The lemon was in blossom, and shimmered in
    between,
Glowed the gold of the orange and the olive's flash
    of green;
I could see them from the waters that rippled blue
    and bright
On the Bay of San Diego in the golden morning
    light.

On the billows' far horizon I saw a white ship sail,
And backward o'er the hills stretched the world-
    wearied trail;
But the ship lured me not that beckoned to the main,
And the trail was not for me, though with gold it
    were lain.

There was no road for me wheresoever it might lay,
Wheresoever over land or the sea it stretched, that
    day;
All the voices of the world died and faltered, though
    they called,
When the Bay of San Diego held my soul, dream-
    enthralled.

'Tis still as God has made it in the gladness of His
     dreams,
With the never-ending Summer that forever o'er it
     gleams,
The mystic seas beyond it in the sunlight's golden
     fire,
And the Bay of San Diego in the Land of Heart's
     Desire.

THE CALL OF CALIFORNIA

Of old she called with her lips of song,
    She called with her breath of musk
From peaks where the sunlight lingers long,
    And the vales in the purpled dusk;
She called to the seas with their tides of tang,
    To the ships of the far-off fleet,
And they came in the lure of the song she sang,
    With their white sails, to her feet.

So, like a mother with bursting breast,
    She claimed the brood of the seas,
And the flaming lips of her wild love pressed
    Upon them, about her knees;
She crooned them to sleep on her bosom fair,
    Where their happy hearts were lain;
And they basked in her smile, above them there
    Like their old, warm skies of Spain.

With cheeks of olive and eyes of night,
        They laughed in her glad caress,
And she gave them her Land of the Living Light
        For their wandering feet to press;
She gave them her Land of the Sun and Shine,
        Where the seas and the deserts part;
And they brought their gifts of the fig and vine,
        And wound them around her heart.

Yet, oft in the light of the mellow moons
        From the jaspered heavens hung,
'Mid the tinkle of soft Castilian tunes
        And bells from the Missions rung,
She dreamed of her bounty brimming o'er
        With its largess of field and plain,
And then from the sweep of the sunlit shore
        Her fond lips called again.

Again she called, and from far away,
        Over desert and mountain keep,
In lands where the wind-swept prairies lay,
        And the ice-clasped torrents sleep,
They heard her voice, like a golden chime,
        And in dreams they saw her rise
From golden streams in a golden clime
        'Neath the blue of faithful skies.

21

Then forth from the toil of grudging field
    And their grinding marts they fled,
While the good ship Argo sailed, new-keeled,
    Where the long sea journey led;
And anon through forests and wastes they fared,
    Over trackless plain and hill,
And many a blood-stained trail they dared
    To the Voice that called them still.

They came, and she dowered with spendthrift
        hands
    The hopes of their wildest dreams;
She flung at their feet the golden sands
    That slept in her shining streams—
Saxon and Teuton and Celt that trod
    The paths of her treasured springs,
With shoon of silver their feet she shod,
    And clothed them in robes of kings.

So hath she called with her lips of song,
    Of old, with her breath of musk,
From hills where the sunlight lingers long,
    And the vales in the purple dusk;
And so, from her soul's unwearied love,
    Rings the voice with its olden thrill—
From the seas below and the skies above,
    She is calling, calling still.

FEAST OF THE FLOWERS

[*La Fiesta de Las Flores*]

They came from the dewy meadows
    Down to the roaring street,
Down to the heart of the crowded mart
    Where the dusty highways meet;
They came from the hills of glory,
    From many a sunlit lea,
And up from the broad campagna
    That stretches to the sea.

Upland and sheltered canyon,
    Where the laughing waters fall,
Field and fell and the woodland dell
    Where the wild birds pipe and call;
From the magic groves of wonder,
    And hedges swept with flame,
Sweet with the dews of morning,
    Kissed of the sun, they came.

Flower and bud and blossom,
  Light of the hill and plain,
One fair morn of the sun god born
  And the song of dancing rain;
Nursed to petal and glowing leaf
  By winds of the West and East,
We plucked them from their scented beds
  And brought them to the feast.

Down to the feast we brought them
  Where the mart-browned city waits,
On a dream-wrapt day of glowing May,
  To the guest within the gates.
To the wandering feet of the stranger
  Far from his wintry skies,
Flower and bloom to the feast we brought
  To gladden his longing eyes.

Soft sang the heart of the city
  When the blossoms wrought their spell—
From fields and fen on the haunts of men
  The odorous breezes fell.
The stranger dreamed within the gates,
  And the guest from far away
Full feasted then on the red-lipped South,
  With her laughing eyes of May.

They feasted full on her beauty,
    Her brows as the lilies fair,
The lotus pressed to her warm, soft breast,
    And the roses in her hair.
They drank the kiss from her dewy mouth—
    And her breath of perfume yet
Will follow anon in the haunting dreams
    Their hearts can ne'er forget.

SAN FRANCISCO

[*1906*]

Night with its revel and its song,
    Night with the lights agleam—
And some sat with the festal throng,
    And some lay down to dream.

Some they quaffed life's purple wine
    And watched its bubbles play,
And some before a cloistered shrine
    Bent low their heads to pray.

And over all who, staying late,
    Kept tryst with good or ill,
The sea fogs through the Golden Gate
    Crept white on bay and hill.

Soft and white the sea fogs lay
    On hill and wave and shore,
While yet, before the break of day,
    One grim hour waited more.

One grim hour more and then unbent
  The battle guns of hell,
And from the hills the veil was rent
  Where white the sea fogs fell.

Dead failed the morning wind that fills
  The galleon's eager sail,
While yet the city's tumbling hills
  Were rocked as in a gale.

Steeple and tower and stately mart,
  Shrine and the lair of lust,
Like toppling cards were flung apart
  And crumbled in the dust.

Some to grasp her trembling knees
  From blasted altars came,
Some with Christ's bitter agonies,
  And some with cheeks of shame;

Moan of the stricken hearts that rushed
  To dust and flame-swept sky,
Till all the seven seas were hushed
  And stricken with the cry.

That day the world forgot to hate,
  To her its tears were sped,
The Keeper of the Golden Gate
  Who wept above her dead!

*　　*　　*　　*

O yesterday and yesteryear,
　　Deep in the dust ye lie,
Dried and forgotten is the tear,
　　Forgotten is the cry.

Up from the ashes of the past,
　　From sorrow and travail,
She greets again the bending mast,
　　She greets the singing sail.

Steeple and tower she lifts anew,
　　With dauntless heart of old;
New-born she greets the skies of blue
　　Where gleam the Gates of Gold.

From thrice her seven hills again,
　　Ringing and sweet and clear,
O'er sunlit seas and stretching plain
　　She sends her song of cheer.

Within her heart the blood beats warm,
　　Her great soul leaps elate—
God save her so, safe from all harm,
　　The Keeper of the Gate!

A PRAYER FOR RAIN

"And also I have withholden the rain from you."

Lord, see'st Thou not, beside the way,
 The drooping flowers
That, week by week and day by day,
 Cry for Thy showers?

Hear'st Thou not the plaintive song
 The wild birds sing,
That in the withered woodlands throng
 With dusty wing?

The bare, brown hills, the blanching plains,
 The silent vale,
They fade and sicken for Thy rains,
 In sore travail.

The wild folk of the forest keeps
 Wail in the night,
And, 'neath the loam, the poppy sleeps,
 Shut from the light.

29

Lord, in Thy wide-flung, bending sky
    Afar there broods,
Where veiled and mist-swept oceans lie,
    Thy cloud-pent floods;

Send Thou from thence the singing rain,
    The laughing streams,
On this dear land of hill and plain
    Thou mad'st of dreams—

This land of dreams Thou mad'st so fair,
    So fair and sweet,
Set like a jeweled footstool, there
    To rest Thy feet.

The earth will blossom at Thy word—
    Oh, speak it, then;
We ask it for Thy mercy, Lord,
    In Thy dear Name.   Amen.

"BACK YONDER"

Away Back Yonder the wintry winds are chill,
In a winding sheet of snow lies the valley and the
  hill,
The patient cattle huddle in the shelter from the
  storm,
And the folks are all housed in 'round the fire, keep-
  ing warm;
It's a hard time they're having, and it sets a man to
  ponder
How glad he ought to be that he's not Back Yonder.

I get to thinking of them, often, when alone,
Here with the birds and the bees' happy drone,
The flowers and the sun and the land with poppies
  gay;
Somehow, through it all, my thoughts backward
  stray,
And I catch myself a-dreaming of the old place, and
  wonder
If the skating's like it was when I lived Back Yonder.

I wonder if they gather in the cold, crispy night,
With the moon's flooding glory on the fields still
    and white,
The lusty-throated boys and the laughing, rosy girls,
Their bright eyes dancing through their tantalizing
    curls,
While coasting's at its best and the ice is gleaming
    under
The bobsleds a-whizzing on the hills Back Yonder.

I think I see the old folks gathered in the glow
Of the hearthstone's warmth that once I used to
    know,
The brown jug of cider of Nature's wholesome brew
And the spoils of the orchard where the luscious
    apples grew.
I think, and I think, till I've half a mind to squander
The last cent I've got on a trip Back Yonder.

But, of course, it's only dreaming, I wouldn't really go
Back to the howling winds, the blizzards and the
    snow,
Away from the flowers and the sun and the bees,
The balm in the air and the sunny days like these;
But I can't help knowing, as far away I wander,
There are other kinds of joys—and they're way Back
    Yonder.

THE GOLDEN GATE

Green Tamalpais, starward swung,
    Brown hill and harbor isle,
O winding rivers, inland flung
    Where sea-lured valleys smile,
I see you from the waters wide,
    I see you watch and wait
The wandering sail, the running tide,
    That win the Golden Gate.

I see you watch and wait, as when
    In quest of Monterey,
Swart old Don Gaspar and his men
    Looked on you first, that day;
I see you watch in mist and sun,
    As when the Spaniard bore
In from the sea his galleon
    Where ship sailed ne'er before.

Footsteps a-many trod since then
    The old Franciscan Trail—
Since swart Don Gaspar and his men,
    Since Juan de Ayla's sail.
From every trail, from every sea,
    With eager hearts elate,
They wandered with what gods there be
    To seek the Golden Gate.

Far from the gates of dawn they came,
    Far from the lands of morn,
Far from the distant sunset's flame,
    And 'round the stormy Horn.
And all the roads, 'twas there they met,
    Where bay to ocean spills,
And there the wanderers' tents were set
    On thrice the seven hills.

The brown-robed Padres pray no more
    In cowl and sandal shoon
When falls on golden sea and shore
    The silver of the moon.
The Argo's rotted keel is laid
    Deep in the harbor's waves,
And they who wrought and they who prayed
    Sleep long in silent graves.

Yet, as of old, the running tide
    Thrills through the Golden Gate,
The rivers seek the ocean wide,
    The brown hills watch and wait.
The stars on Tamalpais gleam,
    The lights flash out to sea,
And this is still the wanderer's dream
    Where'er his path may be.

WHEN COMES THE YULE-TIME

Perhaps some one was thinking of me in another country.
—Robert Louis Stevenson

When comes the Yule-time of the year,
    With fall of eve and dawn of morn,
'Tis then my dreams fly far from here
    To seek the hills where I was born.
'Tis then the scenes I used to know
    Call to my soul with hungering cry—
Mine own white valley in the snow,
    My river and the starry sky.

Here round me lies the flower-flamed land
    That knows no winter's sore travail,
'Tis welcome-warmed of heart and hand,
    And kindly with good friends and hale;
And yet, and yet, oh, heart of me,
    When on the year the Yule days come,
'Tis then one far white land I see—
    Mine own land and the hills of home.

Tonight, with dreams of long ago,
      I'll walk the well-loved paths of yore,
Across the moonlit fields of snow,
      Braving the winds from door to door;
And I shall see the glad surprise
      In faces fond that used to be,
As from their Christmas fires they rise
      With wide flung arms to welcome me.

So shall I sit the hours that pass,
      The places loved and lost among,
Still as of old, with pipe and glass,
      As once when life and love were young;
And I shall hear the North wind blow
      That calls me now with haunting cry
To mine own valley in the snow,
      My river and the starry sky.

DREAMERS OF GOD

The sesqui-centennial of the Founding of
Mission San Buenaventura

The loveliness of Spring was on the world,
    Her carpets spread on hill and vale in flame,
Her banners of wild blossoms all unfurled,
    When here the wandering sons of Francis came.
Brown hands that bore the Living Torch afar
    With canticles of song on paths they trod,
New suns to seek, and always one fixed star,
    And in their hearts the endless dreams of God.

Brown-robed and sandal-shod they fared;
    Their shallops knew the tides of every sea,
Desert and plain and wilderness were dared
    To blaze new trails that reached to Galilee.
Until, at last, they found a sunset shore,
    The last horizon of their eager quest,
Where Christ, their God, was never known before,
    And East began, and ended was the West.

Here in the silent sun-swept vales they strove
    And set the plow among the watching trees,
Sage and mesquite upturned to make a grove
    For golden apples of Hesperides.
Against the hazard of the seldom rain
    They lured the waters of the distant hills
To flow in succor on their fields of grain;
    And there was music in the singing rills.

Against the sky they flung the domes and towers
    Of church and hospice, rising one by one
In dreams of beauty set in arbored bowers
    Of vine and fig tree joyous in the sun.
The anvil rang its challenge to the morn,
    The whirring looms wrought all their magic spells,
And on the hills the shepherd wound his horn
    In answering echo to the Mission bells.

Thus did they work their wonders when they came,
    Before whose steps the pagan gods were fled,
And naked men stood clothed against their shame,
    And they that hungered were with manna fed.
The joy of work, the peace of God was here
    Between the starlit hills 'neath summer skies,
And Christ was throned in temples that were dear
    And loved and holy in His eyes.

Here are their footprints in the desert sands
    That time still treasures from its wreck and loss;
And here is memory of their tireless hands—
    The brown-robed wanderers of the Cross.
The sea remembers and the hills still know
    The olden trails their sandaled footsteps trod
Who swung Christ's fragrant censers, long ago,
    And wrought in beauty as they dreamed of God.

THE CITY OF OUR LADY

[*La Ciudad de Nuestra Senora*]

Of old on the ancient highways,
    When the Golden Land was young,
When down from the Mother Mountains
    To the Mother Sea were flung
Hill and meadow and valley
    With sun and flower aflame,
Sandaled and cowled and eager,
    The brown Franciscans came.

Brown-robed, cowled and sandaled,
    In the lure of a deathless dream,
They reared the new Pueblo
    In the curve of a silver stream;
In call of the mighty mountains,
    And seven leagues from the sea,
They hailed from happy thresholds
    The Queen that was to be.

Fair grew the little Princess,
　　Bonnie and fair and strong,
Her robes the sunset's purple,
　　Her homage the reaper's song.
But ever she longed for the ocean
　　Where the tides of wander be—
Ships and the brown-cheeked sailors,
　　Lure of the calling sea.

She heard the gray gulls calling,
　　And, league by league, she crept
Down to the crooning waters,
　　While others dreamed and slept—
Down where the sailors waited
　　With sails and pennants furled,
And ships with bright gifts laden
　　From harbors of the world.

Down from the Mother Mountains,
　　From lomas and sunlit leas,
Down to the shores of glory
　　And the Mother of the Seas,
Where the old, swart Pablodores
　　Bore sheaves of the harvests home,
Now the Queen of Cities rises
　　With spire and crowding dome.

Queen of the regal cities,
    With banners flung to the sky,
To the caravans she beckons,
    Where trails of the morning lie;
Afar to the tumbling waters,
    Where the tides of wander be,
She answers, with glowing havens,
    The hail of the ships at sea.

FRAY JUNIPERO

A fallen roof beside a tawny trail,
  A moldered cross upon a haunted hill,
And, out at sea, ghost of a ragged sail—
  These hold fond memories of him still.

Cities are builded where his sandals trod,
  Yet not forgotten in the din and greed
Is he who won so fair a land for God,
  Whose faith the heathen from the darkness freed.

A thousand vales with deathless bloom aflame,
  A thousand mountain peaks white-capped with snow,
Still love to speak the gray Franciscan's name
  Who came to California—long ago.

The newer race that destiny has thrust
  Where he with dauntless tread was first to fare,
Lifts up his ruined altars from the dust,
  And sets again the lost lights glowing there.

He won for God the fairest land of all—
  And now, where bright a well-loved river leaps,
And lark and linnet to the sunrise call,
  At peace among the ancient tribes he sleeps.

THE GREEN WAY TO MONTEREY

Green is the way to Monterey,
And once, upon a wandering day,
With breath of mist and flash of sky,
My feet were where the green ways lie;
My soul unleashed, my heart at play,
Upon the road to Monterey.

All in the morning's golden glow
I came by holy Carmelo
Where whispers still its silvery stream
Like voices from an ancient dream,
And through the haunted silence beat
The long-hushed tread of sandaled feet.

Dream-wrapped in memory's mystic spell
I rang the rusted Mission bell,
And called to hill and vale and sea
To give again their dead to me—
The brown-robed priests, the altar lights,
The hosts of dark-eyed neophytes.

45

I called the dead years forth to free
Their dust-thralled feet to trudge with me.
So, fared as comrades with me, then,
Fair women and brave riding men.
By wood and dune that dream-kissed day,
They passed with me to Monterey.

Blithe were the green ways then that told
The gladness of the days of old;
From chaparral with flocks athrong,
Uprose the Indian herders' song,
And ringing scythes, with laughter blent,
From fields where dusky toilers bent.

Madre de Dios! Keep for me
My dream of hill and sky and sea—
The green ways where my path was set,
The gay guitar and castanet,
And stars that hailed, at close of day,
The sunset roofs of Monterey.

WELCOME

[*In honor of the presence in California of the Governors of the States of the United States, July, 1933*]

Welcome was here in the old days of Spain
For every stranger, came he soon or late
By inland trails or from the rolling main
With white flung sail to win the Golden Gate.
Soft speech was here that bade him long to stay—
And, must he go, to speed him on his way.

Welcome was here with bright and lingering glow
Of happy care-free days of Mexico.
The welcome still that bade the stranger bide
Long past the stirrup cup and dusk of night,
Heedless of dawn or fall of eventide
And pageantry of stars, however bright.
All doors were open, every table spread,
And ever, everywhere a waiting bed.

Nor yet was welcome from our bright land fled
When days of Spain and Mexico were sped,
And silent in their gray and crumbled towers
Bells of the Missions were no longer rung
With memories of lost and happy hours
When life and love and all the world were young.

Till when—the Golden Fleece their quest—
Came over plain and desert from afar
The Bald Eagle's brood, flown from its nest,
To set aflame an Empire's restless dreams,
Their campfires' glow upon our golden streams.

Songs of a newer race from minaret
And snow-crowned peaks and sunset sea
Hushed strummed guitars and castanet
With the wild sagas of our destiny.
Yet were old welcomes left us still, nor cast
From clinging memories of a mellowed past.

Here is the welcome still, the same fond hail
That greeted from the sea the wandering sail,
And from the plains the dusty caravan
That flung the Flag across the span
Of the wide continent, from sea to sea,
Daring white mountain peaks and desert gates,
That our vast, ocean-guarded land might be
Enfolded in the Sisterhood of States.

For you who keep the covenant and the scroll
The law and compact of old days and new,
Here where Pacific's tides and billows roll,
The old, fond welcome waits, elate, for you.

For you, the sea, the hill and valley calls—
Yosemite's white misted waterfalls,
Sequoia's groves of immemorial trees,
Our stately cities with their busy marts—
The ultimate West and all its destinies
Embrace you now and fold you in our hearts.

OTHER POEMS

THE PIPERS

The pipers off to the wars are gone—
　　But not the pipers I knew,
For, they are dust now, every one,
　　And dust are the pipes they blew.
　　　　Old and gray,
　　　　They are long away
　　Under the sod and the dew.

They used to play on their pipes for me
　　When I was a little lad;
They came with the bluebird and the bee
　　When earth with the Spring was glad.
　　　　Soft and low
　　　　I heard them blow;
　　And many a lilt they had.

They were as kind as Japheth and Shem
　　To the naked world on their way;
And they wrought to lure me away with them,
　　In the dusk, at the close of day—
　　　　The road for their feet,
　　　　And their pipes were sweet—
　　And I was a fool to stay.

I was a fool to stay behind,
　　Bound to the wheels of the mart,
When the pipers fared on the roads that wind
　　Into the green world's heart,
　　　　Never a care
　　　　Or burden to bear,
　　And neither a horse nor cart.

Sun and rain on their pathways fell,
　　There was no dust of the street.
I was a lad and they loved me well,
　　But the tether was on my feet;
　　　　'Tis on me still,
　　　　And I have no skill
　　To make the pipes blow sweet.

THE CANDLES

Into the hush of an old gray church,
    One day, when I went in,
I saw men come with shuffling feet,
    Dragging their loads of sin;
Dragging the burdens of their souls,
    As I was dragging mine;
And I heard a soft bell tinkle thrice;
    I saw the candles shine.

There is a niche in that old church
    Where many a footstep lags,
'Twas thronged with beggars when I came,
    Beggars in tattered rags.
One poor candle they had to burn,
    One candle, and that was all,
To light the face of the Mother of Christ
    Painted upon the wall.

Forth they stretched their eager hands,
　　As there, in the sudden stir,
I flung my pockets out to them
　　To plead for my need with her.
I gave them silver, I gave them gold,
　　While they mumbled blessings low,
Lighting a hundred candles then
　　That set the niche aglow.

They pressed their lips against her feet,
　　They kissed her garment's hem;
They sent the holy Mother of God
　　Begging to God for them.
And one, more grateful than the rest,
　　His face a glory to see,
Drew me down to my bended knees
　　And set a candle for me.

They sent her begging through heaven wide
　　For their sore needs and mine—
I heard a soft bell tinkle thrice,
　　I saw the candles shine;
My heart within me grew as light
　　As the rags the beggars wore,
And the tender eyes of the Mother of God
　　Followed me to the door.

ROMANY

The King hath his castles,
    And his wide lands in fee,
Yet the mountains shut them in
    And they end at the sea.
But the gypsy, oh, the rover,
    With every wind that's blown,
He tramps the whole world over,
    And claims it as his own.

By the bright, singing waters,
    And every slope of green,
O'er all the rising hills
    And the fields that lie between,
With his brown brood he wanders,
    And his light heart athrill,
And the world is his to squander
    And to barter as he will.

The rich man in cities
    He counts his store of gold,
Yet it rings not with music,
    And the touch of it is cold.
But the gypsy mints the treasure
    Of golden days of sun,
And spends it without measure,
    Nor reckons when 'tis done.

He follows where the swallow
    Its wing southward dips,
He is back with the robin,
    And the song upon his lips.
With his feet for the clover,
    And the stars above him dim,
Oh, the Romany, the rover
    And the glad heart of him.

MY CHRISTMAS FIRE

When I shall light my Christmas fire,
　　High in a quiet hill,
Ere yet is tuned the star-voiced choir,
　　And holy night is still—
Then as the bright flame leaps and streams
　　The deep-heaped fagots through,
I'll have my golden store of dreams,
　　And one will be for you.

There will be many a dream to come
　　And sit the night with me,
Like wanderers returning home
　　From shores of many a sea;
From far-flung trails of rain and sun,
　　On wings that never tire,
They'll come, returning, one by one,
　　To seek my Christmas fire.

And, ready at my hand, shall be
    For each loved dream I name
A fagot of the brushwood tree
    To warm me with its flame;
Fagots of brushwood heaped above
    The hearthstone's ruddy hue;
And, fragrant as the breath of love,
    There will be one for you.

For, lonely were the night and all,
    And lonely life would be,
If in my dreams you would not call
    Across the world to me.
Yet I shall have my heart's desire—
    A dream of you to fill
An ingle at my Christmas fire,
    High in the quiet hill.

PICARDY

[*1918*]

It is a land of rivers,
    But the rivers now are red;
A green land of living things,
    But now 'tis black and dead.
A song was on the winds from sea
    That in the poplars stirred;
Now, in the fields of Picardy,
    A song is never heard.

It was an olden battle place,
    Of spears and clashing blades,
And from its towers the Hermit cried
    The Templars' old Crusades,
It is a place of ancient wars
    Where France was sore beset;
But Time had healed its bloody scars,
    And taught it to forget.

Yet, now again the meadows
     Deep rent and bloody lie,
The pall of death o'er Picardy
     Has blotted out the sky.
Hell's wrath has felled its penciled spires
     And crushed its stately domes;
It is a land of funeral pyres
     Whose embers once were homes.

Once more the Hun has sallied
     To slake his savage wrath,
And, as of old, 'tis Picardy
     That bars his murderous path.
O, gentle place of toil and dreams,
     O, loved of all fair lands,
Hushed are again they singing streams,
     And dimmed thy golden sands!

Lord God, the Hun stood insolent
     Before Thy great white throne,
And now an outraged world he dares,
     Red-handed and alone.
Yet shall this grim hour be his last,
     Shattered his lance shall be;
Broken and spent he shall be cast
     Down to the nether sea.

Then shall the fields be green again,
    And there shall be a song
Where all the stately poplar trees
    Beside the rivers throng.
And they shall come from many lands,
    In rain and sun and shine,
To Picardy, where Freedom's hands
    Have built her dearest shrine.

THE GRAY ROAD OF SORROW

The world has many a road for the feet of you and
    me,
They cross the winding hills where the winds are
    blowing free,
They dip down the valleys, through many a place
    they're cast,
And the gray road of sorrow, oh, we come to it at
    last.

We come to it at last in the mists and sighing rain,
And though we leave it oft the whiles, we come to
    it again;
We come to it again with the sighing rains that fall
On the gray road of sorrow that loves and lures us all.

Once I thought to never walk that gray road hedged
    with yew,
Nor ever did you think to come, if I can read you
    true.
'Twas then that life was blossomed fair, our blood
    with youth aflame,
Yet I found you on the gray road when first to it
    I came.

64

I found you in the sighing rain, beside the hedge of
    yew,
With the trouble dim upon your eyes that once were
    dancing blue,
The trouble deep upon your head, the hot tears on
    your cheek,
And your lips that could but tremble with the word
    you could not speak.

And yet, oh, heart of me, as we wander down the
    years,
We fear it less and love it more, that gray road of
    tears—
The gray road of sorrow with its whispering yew
    and rain,
Its heartaches of memory, its trouble and its pain.

For, trod we ne'er the gray road, but always laughed
    along
The paths of the primrose and the sunlit trails of
    song;
Had we walked but where the happy throngs of
    mirth and pleasure go,
The throb of the gray road we had not learned to
    know.

And it is not when laughter and lilt of joy and song
Ring down the way of roses, where the gay and
    happy throng,
That life has most to give us, but it is when falls
    the rain
On the gray road of sorrow with its heart-break and
    pain.

THE GREEN GLEN OF GLENTIES

The green glen of Glenties, the mountains behind it,
    The blue sky above and the wild seas below,
'Tis far on the way and the road's hard to find it,
    But still 'tis the road that I'm weary to go.
'Tis the road I shall fare when free from the tether,
    Though highways and byways to cross me may
        throng;
Some day from the hilltops all purple with heather,
    I'll look on the green glen that waited so long.

It's little I thought when at night 'round the fire,
    Your hands in my hair as I curled on your knee,
The long years would pass and the laverock tire
    In the green glen of Glenties still waiting for
        me;
It's little I thought with my arms clung about you,
    I would wander the years through the sun and
        the rain,
And come, at the end, to the green glen without you,
    And sit by the Aeny and call you in vain.

And yet, well I know, at the white gate of Heaven,
    You'll hear the deep cry of my soul in its pain,
And you'll say to the Keeper: "Oh, let me be given
    This one day on earth in the green glen again;
For my wanderer is there, who to wander was ready,
    He fared with the sun and the Winter's cold
        blast,
Mine own 'Shawn-ne-Feepa,' my wee sleepy laddie,
    In the green glen of Glenties he wanders at last."

You'll not leave me alone; you will come like the
    sighing
    Of the breath of the glen in the blossoms of sloe,
And I'll rise from the clover, where low I am lying
    To kiss the dear sod that your feet used to know.
And not as I knew you, O fond heart and tender,
    But fair as they told me you were, at the dawn
You'll trip through the dew in youth and in splendor,
    Your cheeks like the roses, your step like the fawn.

Tis far on the way and the road's hard to find it,
    Yet, sometime, at last, on a morning in Spring,
I shall see the green glen and the mountains behind it,
    And sit by the Aeny and hear the thrush sing.
But when that day comes 'tis tears will be near it,
    Like tears that would fall through lilts of your
        song,
That none knew as I. And again I shall hear it
    In the green glen of Glenties that waited so long.

THE SHIP O' DREAMS

The Ship o' Dreams, it sails afar
Where moonlit isles of lotus are,
And round its prow the soft seas break
And croon and whisper in its wake,
But all the guides its sailors see
Are stars of faith and memory.

Bound outward, with the gentle wind,
The shores of care are left behind,
The mart's loud, jarring noises die,
Faint falls its challenge and its cry;
The moan of pain, the drip of tears,
They fail and falter on our ears.

Starboard and port, from rail to rail,
'Tis with our heart's best loved we sail;
The wanderers from the rooftree fled,
The lost ones whom we mourned as dead,
They crowd the decks, and, unafraid,
We watch the golden anchors weighed.

Forth fare we then, with lute and lyre,
By lands of hope and heart's desire,
Past blossomed slope and flowered plain,
Where rise our castles built in Spain;
And peace is there, and o'er us gleams
The sky that folds the Ship o' Dreams.

THE LONG ROAD HOME

It was ever the long road, the long road home,
'Tis long for the bare feet that in the twilight roam,
'Tis long for the sailor who is far away at sea,
But it never was the long road that now it is to me.

Once 'twas just a mile or so, yet in the evening gloam,
When the bee fled the clover and I heard the call of
    home,
When the bird's drowsy head beneath his wing was
    curled,
The long road home was the longest in the world.

And many is the time, in the years that followed fast,
I sat with the stranger by his alien hearth, at last,
With the fisher by the sea and the hunter in the fen,
And many were the miles that I had wandered then.

Still, then it was no matter, for never came the day
That I could not wander back—'twas well I knew
    the way—
With the hunger in my heart and memory aflame,
Though long was the road I could trudge it as I came.

Yet now the hills may beckon and the bright trails
      bend,
But no more they beckon me on the road that has
      no end;
In vain shall I yearn for the welcome at the door
On the long road home, for home is there no more.

HOME CAME THE SAILOR

[*John Paul Jones, dead, from France*]

Home came the Wanderer
    Across the tumbling sea,
Home came the Sailor,
    And the Prince of them was he;
The Prince of all the sailormen
    That ever whipped a mast,
And he sailed to many a harbor,
    But home he came at last.

Home he came at last,
    When sailed the stately fleet,
But silent on the deck he lay,
    The flag his winding sheet.
The surf was at the rudder,
    The prow was lashed to foam,
But dull his ears and dim his eyes,
    When came the Wanderer home.

Home came the Sailor,
    Across the bounding deep,
Home from his exile long
    And from his aliened sleep.
Long was he lost ashore,
    But they found him there at last,
The Prince of all the sailormen
    That ever whipped a mast.

The flag was his winding sheet
    When home the Wanderer came,
It wrapped him with its silver stars
    And with its folds of flame;
The fairest flag that ever flew
    O'er land or ocean free,
And he it was who flew it first
    Upon the ships at sea.

The first was he to fly it,
    With its azure field of stars,
The first to raise upon the masts
    Its flame of crimson bars,
The first to blaze its victor path
    Around the swinging world,
When on the blood-steeped tides of war
    Its glory was unfurled.

White the waves against the shore,
    The tide it homeward runs,
And hoarse with welcome is the roar
    Of iron-throated guns.
Home again, oh, home again,
    With the stately fleets came he,
The Prince of all the sailormen
    That ever sailed the sea.

THE NAVAJO

At morning, when the red sun leaps
    On desert waste and buttes of sand,
Yonder where yet the cactus keeps
    Its stubborn clutch with deathless hand,
The Navajo's wild song of praise
    Rings out across his wind-blown hill
To thank his gods, in his own ways,
    That he may walk his own land still.

Land of much sun and seldom rain,
    Land of the silence and the light,
Land of the softened, shadowed plain,
    Dim 'neath the starlit paths of night,
Land of great moons that come and go,
    Of hushed arroyos dead and dried,
Serene hath here the Navajo,
    Since years forgotten, lived and died.

Here through the years with plenty filled,
 Or lean with hunger, want and thirst,
Whate'er the gods he worshipped willed,
 With much or little, blessed or cursed,
Still to his own land hath he clung,
 Still on its ancient trails he went,
His spells he wove, his songs he sung,
 Glad in his soul and well content.

Where'er your land may be, or mine,
 Lush with green fields and fertile vales,
Rich with its herds and fat with kine,
 Fair with soft hills and meadowed dales;
Though towering dome and penciled spire
 Up to the skies our hands have thrown,
Yet, in his Land of Heart's Desire,
 The Navajo will seek his own.

Gods of the sun and singing rains,
 Spirits of noon and dusky night
That brood above the desert plains,
 Winged with the darkness or the light,
Your blessings to his scant fields bring;
 Make full his springs to leap and flow;
Make glad the songs his lips shall sing,
 And peace be with the Navajo.

THE WINE OF GLORIETTA

Oh, but to drink of that wild wine
    The winds of morning spill
With balsamed sweetness of the pine
    On Glorietta's hill;
Cool from the caves of dawn it slips,
    Soft with the desert's mull,
And once I pressed it to my lips
    And drank it to the full.

I drank it to the full and more,
    I drank it deep and long,
And, weary though the heart I bore,
    It woke its pulse to song.
It set my care-filled heart aglow,
    It set my heart athrill—
Wine of the wandering winds that blow
    On Glorietta's hill.

Green-garlanded through desert sands
    The Pecos wanders there,
And o'er it many a mountain stands,
    Serene, dream-kissed and fair;
But none, like Glorietta, lifts
    Its crest so high and bold
When low and wan the night star drifts
    Within the dawn's red gold.

And, once upon a wandering day,
    Beneath the tender sky,
On Glorietta's peaks I lay
    And let the world go by;
Above, the blue of heaven bent,
    Below the white sands shone,
And glad in mine own heart's content
    I claimed them for my own.

I claimed them as mine own that day,
    And still I dream them mine,
That hill of glory far away,
    The Pecos and the pine,
The sands asleep in desert drought,
    The sentried peaks updrawn,
With Glorietta of the South
    And the wind's wine at dawn.

MY LAND

My land, mine own land, girt round with misted seas,
Headlands breasting to the winds, and sunlit harbor
    lees,
Running tide and oceans wide, shores of flashing
    green,
Mount and vale, hill and dale, and stretching fields
    between;
Jeweled with the stars of night, bright with dews of
    morn,
O my land, mine own land, the land where I was
    born.

My land, mine own land, the fairest and the best
Of all the lands in all the world, or go you East or
    West;
East or West, or North or South, in rain or sun or
    snow,
You'll find no land like my land wherever you may
    go.
Follow all the running tides and every sea bird's call,
And you will find that my land's the loveliest of all.

Here are roses for your breast and poppies for your
    hair,
Ravished from the heart of Spring—there's many
    another there;
Here are jewels for your brows that like the opal
    glows,
I found them in the forests deep that sleep in winter
    snows;
Here are golden harvest sheaves from Summer's
    scented breeze,
I reaped them in mine own land between the misted
    seas.

Give me the star-crowned hills I know, the valleys
    in the sun,
Fields that hold the patriot's dust where many a
    fight was won,
Rivers sweeping to the sea with crystal flash and
    sheen—
And give me then my staff of sloe, my gypsy cap of
    green,
And you may go what way you will, and come
    again or no,
But, up and down mine own land 'tis wandering
    I will go.

THE GUARDIAN ANGEL

"Whence," said the Soul that in God's great glory
    glowed,
"Came my wandering footsteps here and who guided
    me the road
Past the yawning pits of Hell and the darkness and
    the dread,
The jibes of all the living and the terrors of the
    dead?"

From the ringing choirs of Heaven and the shining
    Cherubim,
They brought the Guardian Angel of his life to
    answer him.
And the Angel's was the face that had haunted all
    his years
When the song was on his lips or his eyes were
    dimmed with tears.

"It was thou," said the Soul, "that made hard my
    days for me
With the dreary curse of toil, and thou wouldst not
    set me free
When the face of Pleasure smiled and its pathway
    glittered near."
"Yea," smiled the Angel, "it was so I led thee here."

THE OLD CHURCHYARD

In the old churchyard, though the sun at morning
    gleams,
They who sleep within its bosom never waken from
    their dreams,
Nor answer when you call them, nor listen when
    you speak,
Nor know you weep above them, and that your heart
    may break.
But still, amid the silence, 'neath the soft, green
    mantled sward,
They slumber on forever in the old churchyard.

Yet, somehow, when the gentle winds across the
    grasses blow,
There is something in its whisper like a voice you
    used to know,
And you dream that, as it passes, every gleaming
    drop of dew
Is a tear that some lost loved one has left behind for
    you;
The soul leaps through the gate that.Death, for pity,
    leaves unbarred
'Twixt you and those that loved you in the old
    churchyard.

Mine own are there, mine own that left me lonely
  long ago,
For whom my heart full long hath cried and wept
  and hungered so;
No stranger sleeps among them all, not one but,
  could he rise,
Would welcome me with all the dear old gladness
  in his eyes.
And I bend my face above them, feeling still their
  love may guard
And cherish him who mourns them in the old
  churchyard.

O, the old churchyard! Tho' I wander o'er the sea
And the farthest league of distance, it is ever near
  to me.
Life brings me no new lesson that can teach me to
  forget
The love that first it brought me, and is the fondest
  yet.
And when the days are ended, and the Night comes
  on unstarred,
There is rest for hearts aweary in the old churchyard.

85

THE LAND OF MEMORIE

It lies beyond the sunset hills,
 Far and beyond them all;
And when the twilight shadows creep,
 I hear its voices call.
I hear its voices calling;
 And, you will come with me,
We will trudge away together
 To the Land of Memorie.

And whither lies the way to go
 I have no need to tell;
The way is by the path of dreams;
 'Tis you that knows it well.
'Tis you that knows the way to go,
 And well I know it, too;
You'll follow where the voices call,
 And I will go with you.

The voices there that call us,
     We knew and loved of old,
We knew them round the firesides
     When winter nights were cold;
The friendly word, the welcome word,
     They kept for you and me
Through sunlit days of gladness
     In the Land of Memorie.

Many a door is open there
     Where beams the kindly smile,
And many an arm in welcome flung,
     That waits for us the while.
And, 'neath the whispering grasses
     Where dim the shadows fall,
There's some who, lying lonely,
     Were the best beloved of all.

'Twill pass and fade, 'twill sink away,
     And we must turn anew
To face the burdens of the day,
     The tasks we have to do.
But in some other twilight hour,
     You'll come again with me,
And we'll steal away together
     To the Land of Memorie.

DRAGA

Draga is dead, who was so fair,
    Her dumb lips 'reft of their luring smile,
Her heart's red blood in her matted hair,
    And splashed on her soft, white hands the while;
Her eyes of glory, that flamed and burned,
    Have veiled their fires of love and hate,
And the bucklered hosts of the foes she spurned
    Stand guard, tonight, at her palace gate.

Tomorrow they'll set the crown she wore,
    With its flashing gems, on a rival's head,
And the realm is safe, they will say, once more,
    It is safe, for Draga, the Queen, is dead.
She is dead, the Queen with the wanton eyes,
    Who laughed to ruin the goodly State;
And low in the cloisters of doom she lies,
    Strong-barred 'gainst envy and fear and hate.

'Twas a far, mad journey, the way she came,
　　Up from plebeian paths, alone,
Trailing her garments of sin and shame
　　To flaunt them forth from the purpled throne;
But farther still is the journey now
　　That she takes in the dark, alone, again,
The cerecloth bound on her snowy brow
　　And Death's gaunt courtiers in her train.

Unshrived, in an outcast grave she sleeps,
　　Near the quiet lanes where, of old, she played;
And the long, dim shade of the spire creeps
　　Where in childhood's hours she sang and prayed.
And you, O Masters, who cast the stone,
　　And speak the word you would have us say,
Will the same word serve at the great White Throne,
　　When she pleads for herself on the Judgment
　　　　Day?

DREAMS OF LONG AGO

From Memory's crowded closet-place, like faded
    leaves, sometimes,
I gather these old dreams of mine and kiss them o'er
    with rhymes,
And my foolish tears upon them will glisten like the
    dew
That used to gem the flowers that the old, sweet
    morning knew.

I know the faded leaf hath lost the balm to soothe
    again,
The heart that smarts from sorrow and dagger thrusts
    of pain,
And I know that every dream of these will only
    bring regret,
But 'tis sweeter to remember than it could be to forget.

So I listen to the murmur of the brook's enchanting
    wave
Singing mystic songs of glory that the distance never
    gave,
And I watch the summer rainbow down the heaven's
    vistas bend,
That vanished like the treasures that were hidden at
    the end.

The birds that sang at morning, the noon-hum of
    the bee,
The trees, the flowers, the waters, they all come back
    to me;
They come like tender glances that made sweet my
    mother's eyes,
And leave me like she left me when she fled to
    Paradise.

THE SAILOR OF GENOA

Westward he turned his daring prows,
    Westward he sailed away,
Strange oceans beating upon his bows,
    And dashing his sails with spray;
Strange winds that whipped the bending spars;
    But never a point he veered,
Though high above him the very stars
    Were strange as the path he steered.

Tempest and storm and snarling sea
    The path that he steered beset,
And the waves that broke to the wind and lee
    No man before had met;
Sky that wrapped him and winds that blew,
    No man had known before,
Yet on he sailed with his scowling crew,
    Straight on to the west he bore.

Westward, westward, till hope went down
   In the black seas' deep abyss
From the hearts of his sailors, scarred and brown—
   From every heart but his.
With fear and curses they turned from him
   And scoffed at his mystic goal,
But fate nor furies could quench nor dim
   The faith of his dauntless soul.

Westward, westward, till one fair morn
   The keels of his wandering fleet
Crept into the shallows the tides had borne
   Around a new world's feet.
Around the feet of the world he won
   From the veiled and pathless seas,
When sailed, in his Spanish galleon,
   The immortal Genoese.

A SONG ALONG THE WAY

Always a little nearer,
  The day of the last farewell,
Ever a little clearer
  The sound of the warning bell;
The shadows closer creeping
  Through fading skies of blue,
Then, where the dead are sleeping,
  We'll lie and rest us, too.

So, as we journey, brother,
  Through days that keep us still,
Let us share with one another
  The road that winds the hill.
If load of pain we carry,
  As we trudge along the while,
By the green fields let us tarry,
  And search them for a smile.

Useless, on weary shoulders,
      The trappings of strife we bear,
And the hate that in us smolders
      Makes hard the way we fare.
Let us cast away the madness
      Of swords with which we fought,
And share alike the gladness
      Love's golden pennies bought.

Breasting the winds together,
      As we trudge the age-worn way,
Peace, with its Summer weather,
      Will light the skies of gray.
And then, with hearts grown fonder,
      Serene with their own delight,
We'll speak in the twilight yonder
      A tender and fond good-night.

VIA SANCTI FRANCISCI

They journey light who ways of Francis go,
No heavy burdens of the heart they know,
No shadows of the soul, no pack of care
To bend them wearily as on they fare.
They have no envy of rich men or kings,
For, "having nothing, they possess all things."

Assisi is on every hill. On every plain
Is Umbria like a sunbeam lain
Shining across the world, its gleam
A joyous wakening of the perfect dream.
And where is need of him, there Francis is—
The Little Poor Man with God's hand in his.

THE EAST WIND

It's a dour wind, the East wind, a dour wind and
      cold;
    Many a time and many a time 'twas so I heard
      them say,
Yonder 'round the fires in the lost land of old,
    Yonder in the lost land that guards the gates
      of day.

Strange I used to think it, strange that they should
      speak
    Ill of the East wind that went with me at play,
As kind to me as any, with its breath upon my cheek,
    Yonder in the lost land that guards the gates
      of day.

They were gray folk that said it, gray folk and wan,
    They trembled like the aspen and shivered in
      the cold;
But warm was my heart and I laughed till break of
      dawn,
    Yonder 'round the fires in the lost land of old.

The gray folk they're gone now, gone this many a day,
No more do they gather at the chimney moaning dree,
But, tonight, 'round my fire, heap the fagots as I may,
The East wind is blowing and it chills the heart of me.

Far lies the lost land; the road that leads from there
Is the gray road of sorrow winding down the exile years,
The gray road of sorrow that I never thought to fare,
With the yew tree for hedge, and its white mist of tears.

Oft in the lost land when huddled 'round the fire,
I smiled to the gray folk and cuddled at their knees;
I told them I would wander to the land of Heart's Desire,
And sail on ships o' dreams across the swelling seas.

'Twas then they'd put their hands upon my tossing hair,
Saying, "God bless the laddie where'er his pathway goes,
God bless you, dearie, wherever you may fare,
And shield you from the East wind when bitterly it blows."

God took the gray folk, they lie in dreamless sleep,
  No more around the fires do they gather as of
    old,
And it's I who from the East wind to seek a shelter
    creep,
  Heaping high the fagots to warm me from the
    cold.

It's a dour wind, the East wind, and so I oft was told;
  Many a time and many a time 'twas so I heard
    them say,
Yonder 'round the fires in the lost land of old,
  Yonder in the lost land that guards the gates
    of day.

A SPRIG OF LILAC

A little sprig of lilac, its fragrance in the air,
And, oh, lonely heart, if we could again but fare
Across the weary miles that we've wandered, to the
    door
Where once bloomed the lilac in the happy days of
    yore!

If time could backward turn o'er the years that are
    so long,
And we could see her standing there and hear her
    lilting song,
Her face with its glory and her lips with gladness
    kissed,
It's little we would care for whatever else we've
    missed.

It's little we would care for the dreary days of pain,
The tears and the loneliness, if she were there again,
Her dear arms to fold us, and her tender eyes aglow,
Beside the bonnie lilac bush she planted long ago.

A little sprig of blossoms, their perfume in the air,
But, oh, the weary heart that cannot forget its care;
The memory-haunted years, and the lilacs 'round the
    door
Where once was the welcome that now is there no
    more.

SNUG HARBOR

It's just a place, Snug Harbor is, it may be here or
    there,
Wherever moons are soft at night and suns at morn-
    ing fair;
It's just a place for sailormen, or yet for you or me,
A shelter from the off-shore winds and winds that
    blow from sea.

There's some that call it Port o' Dreams when dis-
    tant tides they roam,
And some who call it Heart's Desire, and some that
    call it Home;
But let them call it what they will, it's still their
    hearts will yearn
For the peace within Snug Harbor where the lights
    of welcome burn.

There's some that never wander far, but when the
    evening falls
Their ears may hear the cry of home that through
    the twilight calls;
Though rains by day from windy hills upon their
    heads are bent,
At night beside their firesides they sit in warm con-
    tent.

But many a one must toil and strive far on the stormy
    waves,
And many a one must beat the trails where winter's
    tempest raves,
And 'tis the hearts of them that dream, through dark-
    ness and the cold,
For the shelter of Snug Harbor and the welcome
    lights of old.

O wanderer on the ancient seas or trails of exiles new,
Come back and I will heap the fire with blazing logs
    for you;
I'll wrap you in my morning cloak and set the room
    aglow,
And watch your glad eyes shining as they used to,
    long ago.

For some they call it Port o' Dreams, and some they
    call it Home,
And some they call it Heart's Desire when far away
    they roam;
But you will call it by the name that still you loved
    the best
When you slept within Snug Harbor upon your
    mother's breast.

THE TOWN O' CROONIN' WATERS

The town o' Croonin' Waters, I dreamed of it today,
Though since my feet have wandered there long
    years have passed away;
Full many a year has passed me since last I wandered
    down
The pathway through the meadows to Croonin'
    Waters town.

God knows how many miles there be that lie 'twixt
    here and there,
How many miles of lifted hills and valleys sleeping
    fair;
But, through the distance fading, they fell and passed
    away,
And back to Croonin' Waters in a dream I walked
    today.

I saw it lying as of old, the shaded streets and all,
Where from the hillside's emerald breast the tumbling
    waters fall;
I heard the waters falling with their old, enchanting
    croon,
And the music of their laughter through the drowsy
    afternoon.

'Twas there that in the days long dead, beside that
    whispering stream,
With boyhood's sunny heart of gold, I used to sit
    and dream,
When life and love and I were young, and when my
    soul was fair
As the white mists of waterfalls that hung above us
    there.

O, town of Croonin' Waters, may God be with it
    still,
The meadows green below it and the mists upon the
    hill,
The shine of sun, the singing rain, the starlight shim-
    mered fair,
And the heart of me that's far away yet longing to
    be there.

THE SEVEN GLENS

The Seven Glens where I was born,
　　'Tis I can see them all,
Green in the Spring with springing corn,
　　And Golden in the Fall.
White they lie with Winter snow,
　　Gray with the misted sky,
And wandering still, where'er I go,
　　For the Seven Glens I sigh.

Kind has the stranger been to me,
　　His hearthstone clean and bright,
Open his hand, his welcome free,
　　His shelter warm at night.
His salt I ate, I broke his bread,
　　And gave his gods their fee,
But ne'er a place I've lain my head
　　Like the Seven Glens to me.

Now, if 'twere so that I could be
    In the Seven Glens once more,
And I could have you there with me
    To pass from door to door;
Trudging around each rolling hill,
    The wayside roofs and fens,
You'd see how well they love me still
    Within the Seven Glens.

Fair is the land where you belong,
    And sweet your hearts and true,
And many is the lilting song
    That I have made for you.
There's many a land that's bright with morn,
    And soft with stars aglow,
But the Seven Glens where I was born,
    'Tis there that I would go.

KINSHIP

Lure of the winding trail,
    Croon of the coaxing sea,
Song of the wind and sail,
    Well were they loved of me.

And I wandered far and wide
    With the gypsy's wide desire,
Till then when you sat beside
    The glow of my roadside fire.

Under the starlit skies
    We sat till the dawn stole in,
And long I looked in your eyes,
    And saw that we two were kin.

Red from the ancient past,
    In our veins the same blood creeps
Of our fathers bent to the mast,
    Who toiled on the windy deeps.

Afar lies the coaxing sea,
    And the trail in the morning dew,
But in vain they call to me
    At the roadside fire with you.

THE RAIN

I woke in the night and thought I heard you calling,
But 'twas another music, 'twas the soft rain falling;
It tripped with lilting whispers from the warm skies
    of Spring,
And it sang me a song like the songs you used to sing.

'Twas the mid-hour of night and the embers in the
    fire
Were cold as your folded hands and dead as your
    desire,
But my heart was warm with memory, it heard the
    beating rain,
And dreamed it was your luring lips that called to
    me again.

Night and the rain and the dead, ashen ember,
These are for me, for me that must remember;
The embers and the rain and the night in shadows
    set,
These are for you, for you who can forget.

THE FOUR ROADS OF MORNING

The four roads of morning 'tis them that I remember,
As now from out the evening fires I watch each
    dying ember;
The long roads, the sunny roads that crossed and
    stretched away,
And the eager feet that waited there when broke the
    golden day.

The long roads, the sunny roads, we saw them wind
    and bend,
And whichever one we chose to take held gladness
    at the end.
There was gladness at the end of them before the
    sun would set.
Oh, the four roads of morning, I see them smiling yet.

The four roads of morning, it's them that I remember,
With the dreams of you to warm me as dies the day's
    last ember;
The dreams of you that warm me, as I light the
    evening fire
With tinder-sticks of memory from the road of
    Heart's Desire.

"YOU ALL"

You all never reckoned when I said good-bye that
    day,
How hard it was to choke the tears and turn and
    go away,
To go away with all the tears welled up, like Sum-
    mer rain
Behind the smile that I put on to hide the hurt and
    pain.
And, as with outstretched hands I stood, when came
    the hour to part,
Oh, you all never knew the dreary hunger in my heart.

Down through the sun-kissed valley, its circled hills
    between,
Down with the winding river through the meadows
    soft and green,
Beyond the waving fields of grain just touched with
    harvest gold,
And the happy scenes of boyhood that I knew and
    loved of old,
Outcast and aliened from it all, as in a dream, I
    passed,
But, oh, dear hearts, 'twas you all I thought of at last.

There's many a winding river and many a sun-kissed
    vale,
On a wandering day, between the dawn and fall of
    twilight pale,
There's many a harvest field of gold and meadow
    soft and green
The two wide tumbling oceans and the lonely seas
    between,
But they never seem the same to me, they never look
    so fair,
And I know it's only just because that you all are
    not there.

THE VALLEY OF DUNLOE

Sometime, when shines the gypsy star
    Deep in the skies and low,
I'll leave dull care behind me far,
    And wandering I will go.
I'll take my gypsy cap of green,
    My old, loved staff of sloe,
And never stop till I have seen
    The valley of Dunloe.

Though up and down the world I went,
    This long and many a day,
'Tis strange that I have never bent
    My wandering steps that way.
'Tis strange, indeed, that, dry or wet,
    With all the winds that blow,
A foot of mine trod never yet
    The valley of Dunloe.

But never other road I'll fare,
	Nor rest content the same,
Until I see the spot from where
	The homesick people came—
The homesick people loved of me,
	'Round firesides of old,
When chimney winds were singing dree,
	And winter nights were cold.

In the valley of Dunloe, they said,
	The primrose fairest grew;
From skies of morning, overhead,
	Rained showers of honeydew;
The lark's song was the sweetest there,
	And oft, I've heard them tell,
That, better there than anywhere,
	The fairies loved to dwell.

'Tis yet the fairest place, by far,
	In all the world, I know;
And so, when next the gypsy star
	Beams from the skies aglow,
The homesick people that I knew,
	When exiled, long ago,
Will see my green cap nodding through
	The valley of Dunloe.

THE PORT O' HEART'S DESIRE

Down around the quay they lie, the ships that sail
    to sea,
On shore the brown-cheeked sailormen they pass the
    jest with me,
But soon their ships will sail away with winds that
    never tire,
And there's one that will be sailing to the Port o'
    Heart's Desire.

The Port o' Heart's Desire, and it's oh, that port
    for me,
And that's the ship that I love best of all that sail
    the sea;
Its hold is filled with memories, its prow it points
    away
To the Port o' Heart's Desire, where I roamed a boy
    at play.

Ships that sail for gold there be, and ships that sail
    for fame,
And some were filled with jewels bright when from
    Cathay they came,
But give me still one white sail in the sunset's mystic
    fire
That the running tides will carry to the Port o'
    Heart's Desire.

It's you may have the gold and fame, and all the
    jewels, too,
And all the ships, if they were mine, I'd gladly give
    to you,
I'd give them all right gladly, with their gold and
    fame entire,
If you would set me down within the Port o' Heart's
    Desire.

Oh, speed you, white-winged ship of mine, oh, speed
    you to the sea,
Some other day, some other tide, come back again
    for me;
Come back with all the memories, the joys and e'en
    the pain,
And take me to the golden hills of boyhood once
    again.

SHIPS AND CARAVANS

Moon-vales splashed with flowery light;
    Hills in mottled tans;
And over them, by day and night,
    Creak the caravans.

Blue-green water of the deep
    That to the west star dips;
And on the tossing billows sweep
    White sails of the ships.

Comrade once was I with these,
    With ship and caravan,
On tides beyond Hesperides,
    On trails to Ispahan.

Upon the wild and tumbling main
    I had my old desire;
And by a red-roofed hill of Spain
    I built a roadside fire.

To dusks of walled Toledo town
    I climbed with ghosts to be;
And I have been to Carcasonne
    And isles of Innisfree.

So, if no more the kind gods slip
    The tethers from my feet,
If never caravan or ship
    Again with me shall meet,

I have of them my golden dream;
    They have their dream of me
When night falls on a wayside stream
    And morn breaks on the sea.

THE TRINKET

There's a little shop in Genoa
    To which not many fare,
And, now that I remember,
    I bought a trinket there.

A shop of keepsake things it is,
    Or whatever else might be
To catch the eye of lonely men
    Who wander in from sea.

The King was in his palace
    Across the hills in Rome,
The Pope was in the Vatican,
    And I was far from home.

But, never did I tell the King,
    Or make the Pope aware
That I had come to Genoa
    And bought a trinket there.

SHAMEEN RUE

Shameen Rue, 'twas the name we called him,
    (Oh, Shameen Rue and the days of old)
His blue eyes tender with dreams that thralled him,
    His shining hair like the fire o' gold.
Alone with the hearthstone's smoldered embers,
    'Tis many's the time I think of him
And the old, old days that my heart remembers,
    When the past comes back and my eyes are dim.

Glad would I be if I were knowing,
    When they lay me under the sod and dew,
I could carry away to the place I'm going
    The love of the world like Shameen Rue.
It's little I'd care though fortune kiss me
    With kiss of Judas both night and day,
If I knew the old and the young would miss me,
    As he was missed when he went away.

'Tis well I mind how with them, together,
     When gentle hands trimmed the lamps of home,
In the twilight fall of the wintry weather,
     (Long, long ago 'ere I learned to roam)
In rain or storm or the white snow drifting,
     At every door was a hand he knew
Would strive for joy to be first at lifting
     The latch of welcome for Shameen Rue.

How the children flew to his arms to meet him,
     And leaped to answer his cheery call,
And the gray-grown people rose up to greet him—
     'Twas they who loved him the best of all.
To see them then it would well content you,
     As they drew him near to the chimney chair,
And they used to say: "It was God that sent you,
     Oh, Shameen Rue of the shining hair."

I've wandered far, and what good it's done me
     'Twere easy counted and quickly said;
I've food and shelter, and friends I've won me,
     But the best and truest are with the dead.
I've seen great cities with dome and steeple,
     And wondrous women and gallant men,
Yet, better I'd stayed with the kindly people
     And Shameen Rue in our native glen.

I've found the places where life is streaming,
    I watch it passing in power and pride,
But tonight 'tis of Shameen Rue I'm dreaming,
    And the little world where he lived and died.
Yon little world that the hearthstone embers
    Again bring haunting and bright and fair,
With the days and ways that my heart remembers,
    And Shameen Rue of the shining hair.

LITTLE RIVERS

Little rivers that dews have made
    From bramble bushes and forest tree
And morning mists in a grassy glade,
    They are the rivers dear to me.

There is boast of power in mighty streams
    That bear great ships to the waiting seas,
But little rivers are made for dreams
    And the heart's stored treasure of memories.

They know not travail of toil or grief,
    But lightly voyage in sun and shower
The galleon of a fallen leaf
    And bright-hued sails of a wind-blown flower.

They are here and there, and I know them well—
    Better than anyone·else I know
There is blossom of fadeless asphodel
    Wherever the little rivers flow.

THE ROAD TO GALILEE

Rememberest thou the way,
    In sandal shoon He came?
Upon that day, that wondrous day,
    They spoke His holy name.
Hushed were the land and sea
    As with an angel's breath.
It was the road to Galilee,
    That leads from Nazareth.

The path was sere and dried,
    The vines had ceased to cling,
And on the dusty roadside cried
    A bird with broken wing.
To bloom the dead leaves stirred
    Beneath His footsteps pressed,
And from His hand the wounded bird
    Flew to its waiting nest.

Rememberest thou the way
    Of immemorial pain,
Upon that day, that wondrous day,
    He came to weeping Nain?
His pitying touch set free
    The widow's son from death.
It was the road to Galilee
    That led from Nazareth.

As on His way He went,
    The fold's lost sheep to seek,
He healed the arm in palsy bent,
    And kissed the leper's cheek.
And from the city's din,
    Stoned from the shadows, crept
The nameless one He cleansed from sin,
    As at His feet she wept.

With corn was Canaan green,
    Yet waited there no bed
For Him, the outcast Nazarene,
    On which to lay His head.
The road to Galilee
    Must lead Him, wandering still,
Up to the Cross of Calvary
    That beckoned on the hill.

Rememberest thou the hill
    To which, at last, He came?
That wondrous day the world stood still,
    No more to be the same.
No more to victor be
    The grave, nor sting of death.
It was the road to Galilee
    That leads from Nazareth.

THE QUEEN CITY

[Seattle, 1897]

The shelter-craving sea
    Crept to her feet,
The west wind, strong and free,
    In her face blew sweet.
And oft, as the breath of the main
    Her bosom kissed,
She hid in her cloak of rain
    And veils of mist.

The Sailor wandering far
    The trackless deep,
Turned to the steadfast star
    That watched her sleep.
And the dauntless Pioneer,
    Through forests wide,
Blazed the bleak pathway clear
    That reached her side.

They throned her on the hills
    Of changeless green,
'Mid the gleam of mountain rills
    And lakes' soft sheen;
They filled their souls with her name,
    Her love and grace,
And the sons of the four winds came
    To see her face.

Jewels and gems they brought,
    And raiments gay,
Treasures the looms had wrought,
    In far Cathay;
Gifts from the vales and plains
    And marts of old,
And the north from its frozen veins
    Poured out its gold.

Then her wild pulses stirred,
    Her warm heart beat,
She sang that the whole world heard,
    And the song was sweet.
The salt rains swept her lips,
    Still, from the skies,
She laughed to the crowding ships
    Through sunlit eyes.

ROOSEVELT IN THE YELLOWSTONE

[*When President of the United States, Theodore Roosevelt spent a vacation in Yellowstone National Park studying wild animal life. When he was leaving a great herd of Elk followed him, as though in escort, to the Park boundaries.*]

Above him the wild skies bending,
    Beneath him the wastes of snow;
Through the hush of the forest wending,
    And over the bleak plateau,
He rode, with his strong heart glowing,
    In a clime of old, held dear,
And the winds of the West were blowing,
    With the music he loved to hear.

Beside him, with clanking saber,
    The brown-cheeked trooper rode,
Yet, he passed, as friend and neighbor,
    Where the things of the wild abode;
Where the things that people the places
    Of mountain and hill and fen
Were waiting, with kindly faces,
    To welcome the chief of men.

And so that they, too, might render
    Their tribute of love to him,
Forth, then, in their strength and splendor
    From the forests dark and dim,
From the wastes and the gushing fountains
    Like a leaping wave of flame,
The antlered kings of the mountains
    In royal escort came.

Down through the wild wastes riding,
    They followed him over the snow,
By the peaks in the cloud-mists hiding,
    And down to the broad plateau;
And never, in song or story,
    In tourney, or feast, or fray,
Rode King or Khan in his glory
    As this man rode that day.

THE ROUGH RIDERS

[*The unveiling of the Roosevelt Rough Rider Equestrian Statue of Captain William O. ("Bucky") O'Neill, in the Plaza at Prescott, Arizona, July 3, 1907.*]

Souls of rough riding men, the first-born and the last,
Come and gather 'round us from out the storied past,
Come from the field of Monmouth, the red-dyed
    Rapidan,
Come with Putnam and Marion, Stonewall and
    Sheridan;
Far from silent bivouacs that sleep in ancient dust,
Leap again to saddle, unsheath you swords of rust,
List to the bugle ringing clear on the desert sky,
Calling the war-worn troopers that now go riding by.

Come and gather 'round us, souls of hard riding men,
Who fought with swinging sabers, of old, o'er hill
    and glen,
Souls of the strong adventurers who blazed the bloody
    trail
Down from the guns of Lexington to Shenandoah's
    vale;

132

Halt your ghostly riders, your squadrons side by side,
While they ride by who rode, as you, upon a battle tide,
Wanderers of the savage hills and desert's blinding
  plain,
Who spilled their eager hearts against the chivalry
  of Spain.

We'll dream again they're gathered from near and
  far away,
That host that to the Alamo rode down one sun-
  kissed day.
The bronco busters of the plain, the hunters from the
  hill,
The keepers of the rainless wastes that love and lure
  them still;
Brood of the trackless wilderness, swart with desert's
  breath,
Spawn of the brown Southwest whose trails are dim
  with death.
We'll dream once more they're mustered, here 'neath
  skies aglow,
A thousand strong in the rendezvous as then at the
  Alamo.

And as the dust-brown columns sweep on with
  thunder tread,
Full will we fling a cheer for him, the chieftain at
  the head,
A cheer for him the chieftain, who led them on the
  way,

At whose clear call to glory they galloped to the fray,
Him they trailed to victory where flamed the flag
     unfurled,
The one great heart of all best loved of all the world.
We'll lift our hearts to greet him as breaks the vision,
     then,
Of Roosevelt still riding with his rough riding men.

Sing from your throat, O bugle, as they ride forth
     at dawn,
From Caney and Guaysimas and the hill at San Juan;
Turn again, O Memory, with heart that holds them
     dear,
Again their steeds are champing, the hoof-beats
     sounding near;
Home from crimson fights they won, home they come
     at last,
To ride in full review before the spirits of the past,
Here, where one silent trooper waits upon the way
The last rung trumpet call that wakes the Judgment
     Day.

Onward they come in full review, the living and the
     dead,
Troop and the plunging squadron, their leader at the
     head;
And he will halt his charger as all the columns wheel,
Where face to face they stand again—Roosevelt and
     O'Neill.

Up to the Colonel's lips will leap his saber in salute
To him, the well-loved Captain, who sits the stir-
    rups mute,
Smiling as when he answered to freedom's crowding
    roll,
And death flung to the darkness his wild and gallant
    soul.

So shall they come with Memory from near and far
    away,
The host that from the Alamo rode out one sunlit
    day.
Back they come to mountain and desert's shining
    plain,
The living and the gloried dead, the wounded and
    the slain;
Every saddle set once more as when they rode to war,
To strike for a new republic, to die for a new born
    star;
Not a gap in the ranks of dream that sailed the tropic
    sea—
Colonel, Captains and troopers all, home from *Cuba
free*.

So shall they come and pass away as evening's shadow
    falls,
And good-night songs and reveille the singing bugle
    calls,
Leaving this one lone sentry upon the grim plateau

Over the purpled buttes aflame and shifting dunes
    below,
Here in his silent stirrups with desert stars agleam,
Soul of the wild adventure, heart of the deathless
    dream,
One faithful, sun-browned trooper that waits upon
    the way
The last rung trumpet call that wakes the Judgment
    Day.

THE ROOFTREE

Once on a time a strong man hewed
A rooftree for his little brood;
His sinewy hands its rafters reared,
His swinging ax the forest cleared,
'Till orchard-bloom and fields of loam
Smiled 'round it, and he called it Home.

And there, for many a happy day,
He heard his children shout at play,
Or watched them, barefoot, wander through
The clovered meadows steeped in dew;
And, one by one, he saw them fare
Forth from the fold, the world to dare.

Then came a time when 'neath the shade
Of arbors that his hands had made,
They laid him in the soft, cool mold,
His labors done, his story told.
And silence breathed its hush and spell
On that dear place once loved so well.

The rooftree crumbled, spiders wove
Their fairy webs its eaves above;
But yonder, in the world's wild way,
Those who had loved it in their play,
Stopped oft, through days that care beset,
To name it with their heart's regret.

A rich man in his halls of pride,
Through many an hour of longing sighed
For its bright, flowery paths again;
And one who lay in fevered pain
On glory's field, near death's dim brink,
Cried for its sweet, cool springs to drink.

And there was one poor Ishmael,
Who, when his ill-starred fortunes fell,
Turned like a hunted dog at bay,
Backward, o'er many a devious way,
To lay him down with death, care-free,
Once more within the old rooftree.

AFRICANUS TRIUMPHANS

When, out of the chaos, earth was hurled,
 And God's great mandate spread;
When He made the races to fill the world—
 Yellow and white and red—
There was one made black, and the other three
 Seeing him, asked to know
Whence, from what darkness cometh he?
 And whither does he go?

And the black man said God made us free,
 White and black men all,
Yellow or red, whichever we be,
 There shall be no bond or thrall;
But they said his lips had spoken lies,
 For the brand was on his cheek,
And they dulled their ears to his children's cries,
 And the word his tongue would speak.

So, through the ages hath he borne,
    With shoulders bowed to the wheel,
The whole world's burdens and its scorn,
    Its bloodhounds at his heel.
Bound he stood in the palace hall,
    He was chained to the galleyed ships,
Yet, with deathless courage he braved it all,
    With the challenge upon his lips.

Out from the ages, stained and dim
    With curse and wrong and hate,
He comes with the patient heart of him
    Unbent of Time or Fate.
Lash and shackle and gyve and goad
    He bore through grief and dole,
Yet stands at last, from the weary load,
    Erect with dauntless soul.

Never an hour of the countless years
    When the slavers' lashes gleamed,
But through the rain of blood and tears,
    Of his birthright still he dreamed;
Never a night of gloom and pain
    But brought him hope of morn,
With vision of Liberty dawned again,
    And the freedom he lost, new born.

He comes with glory from wars of death
    For the flag that made him free,
He comes from the cannon's thund'rous breath
    That he faced all fearlessly;
He comes with songs his poets sing,
    The pictures his painters drew,
With music the tongues of his pleaders ring,
    And the things that his hands can do.

He comes, my brother, whoever you be—
    Yellow, or white, or red—
In the fair, full light of his destiny,
    With the word that, of old, he said.
Gentle and patient and brave and strong,
    With the faith of his soul unworn,
And the time is past for shackle and thong,
    And the time is past for scorn.

O olden race of the jungle and hill,
    O olden race and strong,
Brave be your heart with the challenge still,
    And glad be your lips with song.
Look up to the glory that flames the skies,
    The gloom of the night is done;
Oh, shout to the morning with victor cries,
    For the long, hard fight is won.

LITTLE GREEN LAND OF IRELAND

Little green land of Ireland,
    Girt by the wild, white waters,
Where are the sons that thou hast borne,
    And where are thy blue-eyed daughters?
Seek thou the seas that lie afar,
    And search through the lands behind them,
And wherever a sail or a trail is seen,
    It is there that thou wilt find them.

Little green land of sorrow,
    On the breast of the white sea lying,
Whose are the voices that call to thee
    When the winds in the glens are sighing?
Voices of exiles are they that speak
    Thy name that still grows fonder,
Wherever they be in the alien lands
    Where their homesick footsteps wander.

Little green land of gladness,
    From Antrim to soft-voiced Kerry,
Thou hast still a foot that's light in the dance
    When the pipes are blowing merry.
On thy lips are yet the lilt and song,
    And the wit that's e'er beguiling
To lure from thine eyes the mist of tears,
    And coax them into smiling.

Little green land of my mother,
    There's a glen in thy warm heart sleeping,
Where a winding river runs to the sea
    With the red, free salmon leaping.
It was there she learned the song of the thrush,
    When the sky was blue above thee,
And as long as that glen lies in thy heart,
    O, little green land, I'll love thee.

PENNSYLVANIA

Home, oh, home, and the name of it
    That we speak on a stranger shore,
And find in our hearts the old love still
    For the days and the things of yore;
The name of it and the love of it
    That nothing can lure away,
No matter how blue the skies that bend,
    Or how fair the paths we stray.
Longing, and backward turning still,
    With memory fond that thrills,
We dream of the sweeping rivers
    And the stretch of the old blue hills.

May is there and the days are fair
    In the Land of the Long Ago,
The wild flowers are in blossom now,
    And the south winds softly blow;
The robin sings and the chewink cries,
    And the thrush is nesting there,

The sunlight sleeps on the fields of corn
　　And the clovered meadows fair;
The mountain rills that flash and gleam
　　In the light of the dewy morn,
They are singing the songs I used to know
　　In the land where I was born.

Orchards bloom on the sunny slopes,
　　The daisy's white in the fields,
And the anvil's music is ringing there
　　From the arm that Labor wields;
Smoke from the grimy marts of toil
　　And the busy hives that glow
With the quenchless fires of Industry
　　Where the tides of Commerce flow;
Wealth of the cities pouring down
　　Where the crowded harbor lies,
And "her name is written in furnace flame
　　On the scroll of midnight skies."

FRIENDS

Friends are like rivers flowing to the sea;
They come and go, yet ever constant be.
And though we wander desert lands afar,
Our hearts are ever where the rivers are.

Friends are like hills against a bended sky;
Though mists may hide them, still we know
    them nigh.
And though we journey far in sun and rain,
The hills we loved will call us back again.

NEXT DOOR

[An incident of the World War]

A long time we haven't been good friends—
    The house next door and I;
And now I've got to go and make amends,
    And put my foolish notions by.
A while ago the morning paper came,
    And, almost at first glance,
I saw, with startled eyes, the name
    Of their boy, dead in France.

I don't know just what to say,
    When I go in to that hushed place
With blinds drawn against the light of day,
    And meet them, face to face.
His mother, his sisters and his dad,
    And he was their only son—
Well, never mind the harsh words we've had,
    That's past now, and I'm done.

We haven't been good friends, and yet
    They couldn't help but see
When the boy left, with eyes all wet,
    He said "Good-bye" to me.
Thank God for that. Maybe they'll know
    How light the grudge he bore;
Maybe they will forgive me when I go
    To bare my heart, next door.

Maybe they'll somehow sense that I
    Would gladly take his place,
And give them back their boy who had to die
    In his glad youth and grace.
France and the Flag—and he so young—
    Death and the war's wild din—
God help me and my faltering tongue,
    Next door, when I go in.

SOLDIER

Soldier, soldier, here you sleep,
    Soldier, here you lie;
Narrow is the bed, and deep,
    And you were young to die.
The crimson tide of war is sped,
    Stilled is the battles' din;
And this is such a darksome bed
    To tuck a soldier in.

It is a darksome bed for you
    Who played the big red game
And under God's vast skies of blue
    Had seen the world aflame.
It is a quiet couch for one
    Who heard the great guns roar.
Soldier, soldier, life is done
    And throbs for you no more.

Yea, youth was flaming in your veins
    To which one bullet sped
And all the grass was reddened stains
    Where you lay with the dead.
Soldier, you were with the slain
    Where Death's black lance was flung.
You fell no more to rise again;
    And, ah, you were so young.

When old men die, what need to weep?
    Their bones have felt the racks,
Their eyes were weary wooing sleep,
    Life's loads were on their backs.
But, soldier, soldier, here you rest
    Shut from the wide blue sky
And life and love. And God knows best.
    And you were young to die.

"THE 'HUNDRED AND FORTY-THIRD"

They were there in the red, red rain;
    The din of battle their voices heard
In the bloody charge with the spent and slain—
    The 'Hundred and Forty-Third.
This one and that one, young and kind,
    Strong and tender and brave, withal;
From the folded hills where the waters wind
    They marched away at the bugle's call.

They marched away on a Summer's day,
    When breath o' morning the grasses stirred;
Brown-cheeked lads that had come from play—
    The 'Hundred and Forty-Third.
Guns ashoulder with bayonets bright
    Shone and gleamed in the sunlight fair.
You've heard of Cold Harbor's bloody fight?
    The 'Hundred and Forty-Third was there.

Just brown-cheeked lads who went away
	At bugle call and the drum's wild thrills,
From their boyish tasks and their boyish play
	By the winding stream in the folded hills.
And Chancellorsville was the next we knew,
	And Gettysburg was the next we heard;
The lads that were many were then but few
	In The 'Hundred and Forty-Third.

'Twas long ago; 'tis another day,
	And the world forgets; but we still mind
When they came from play and marched away
	From the hills afold where the waters wind.
We still remember the noble dead
	Whose last farewell 'twas of old we heard,
And green are the laurels for each gray head
	Of The 'Hundred and Forty-Third.

THE RANSOM

There was one sin that I loved most,
    One wish there was best loved of me.
I gave them to a dead man's ghost,
    To set his poor soul free.

I gave them from my heart's red core,
    And left it seared and gray with pain,
That he might burn in flame no more
    Nor walk the night again.

He met me when the stars were deep;
    His lowly grave near-by was laid.
Oft, 'ere he went with death to sleep,
    In that same spot we strayed.

He met me there with pleading eyes,
    The same fond, tender eyes of old,
And, in my fear and dread surprise,
    My faltering blood ran cold.

He followed me within my door,
    Nor fled till day began to break,
The while he ceased not to implore
    With lips that could not speak.

But when, at length, he went away,
    Full well I knew what was to be,
What ransom it was mine to pay,
    What boon he asked of me.

And so, with heart grown old in grief,
    I went where shone the shrine of prayer,
And plucked my roses, leaf by leaf,
    And left them lying there.

My wayward soul I shrived full clean,
    With knout and lash my flesh I flayed,
In sackcloth, where dim altars lean,
    For his soul's peace I prayed.

But, oh, the dear sin, long enticed,
    Drowned in that dregged and bitter cup;
And, oh, that wild wish sacrificed,
    That then I offered up.

'Twould souls of thrice a thousand save,
    'Twould 'fend a kingdom from God's wrath,
Which, to the dead man's ghost I gave,
    That night he crossed my path.

Long since his happy feet are set
    Upon the shining streets of gold,
But, in his joy, can he forget
    His debt to me of old?

Will he forget when my soul waits,
    And dark my day of troubles fall?
Or will he storm the Jasper Gates
    To help me, when I call?

GRAY MEN OF BATTLE

Blow a note on the bugle,
    Wake a throb of the drum
As down the Springtime highways
    The old gray soldiers come;
Bugle and drum to thrill them,
    And quicken the step that lags;
Bugle and drum and old gray men,
    And the folds of tattered flags.

Room for the war-worn column
    That wavers along the street,
Room for the crutch and empty sleeve,
    And the slow, uncertain feet;
A hush on the shout and clamor,
    As they pass with faltering tread,
The gray men of the battles
    Who pass to seek their dead.

Room for the men of Antietam,
    Where charged their battered lines;
Room for the lions of Malvern Hill
    And the eagles of Seven Pines;
Room for the clanking saber,
    And the foot that once swung free
Through Shenandoah with Sheridan,
    And with Sherman to the sea.

Old and bent in the highways,
    Their tattered flags on the breeze,
Never leaped at the jaws of death
    Such fighting men as these;
Never saw flame of rampart,
    When battle tides ran red,
The like of these old gray soldiers
    Who seek today their dead.

These are the men of Shiloh
    Who pass with footsteps slow,
The steeled brigades that stormed the clouds
    Of Lookout with Fighting Joe.
These are the stubborn legions
    That on Chickamauga hung
When the bugles sang of slaughter,
    And the old gray men were young.

O lingering note of the bugle,
    Throb of the muffled drum,
As down the Springtime highways
    The old gray soldiers come!
Only a few more twilights
    On the wavering ranks and thin,
Then night and folded banners,
    And the sabers gathered in.

THE SADDENED HEART

I need not say that I am sad,
    For every one is so;
The world is for a moment glad,
    And then 'tis full of woe,
And even while we laugh, a tear
Falls through the music that we hear.

The saddest hearts I met today,
    The eyes that sorest wept,
Last night were full of mirth, and gay,
    And changed but while I slept;
But then the sky was bright and blue,
While now it wears a somber hue.

He who, with voice of silvery ring,
    Told me one hour ago
That life was such a happy thing—
    With curses deep and low
Avers that now he does not care
For life or death in his despair.

And thus it is, and thus 'twill be,
    E'en as 'twas long ago.
You need not speak your grief to me,
    With every one, 'tis so;
And you, and I, and all, but tread
Upon the hope that shrouds the dead.

THE TOILER

Smokeless towers and silent wheels,
    Today on the lonely hill,
And the restless hands are folded,
    And the tireless heart is still.

The eyes that pierced the darkness
    Of the very earth are dim,
And of all his wide dominions
    There is only a grave for him.

He walked wherever the toiler
    Had shapen his sturdy tread,
When the scented way of the roses
    Was his, if he cared, instead.

And wherefore hath he striven
    If not for gold and gain?
Did he fashion his wheels of iron
    For torture and human pain?

Answer, O lips that tremble!
    Answer, O tearful eyes
That ask God's peace and blessing
    Upon him where he lies!

Yea, 'twas for you, my brothers,
    With tireless brain he strove,
And the smoke from his grimy towers
    Was the incense of his love.

And after the weary struggle
    No curse falls on his head,
No trail of blood to tarnish
    The blameless life he led.

Peace and farewell, O Toiler!
    God grant that some day shall see
This sad old world as happy
    As your dream would have it be.

SONG

Grieve not to say good night, dear,
    Good night is not good-bye;
And 'though at morning's light, dear,
    Long miles 'twixt us shall lie,
        Sometime I will come back to thee
        As happy as of old to be.

And every lonely day, dear,
    That parts our lives in twain,
At last will pass away, dear,
    And we shall meet again.
        So, why should tears dim thy fond eye?
        'Tis but good night and not good-bye.

We've known full share of pain, dear,
    Of heartache and of tears;
Fond hopes we knew were slain, dear,
    And love grew sick with fears,
        But soon the shadows all will flee,
        And we no more will parted be.

And when you're all my own, dear,
  Like blessings then will fall
The sorrows we have known, dear,
  The loneliness and all.
      So, wherefore tears to dim thine eye?
      Good night, dear Love, but not good-bye.

PRAISE

How art thou praised? By word or look?
    Yet still not so shall I praise thee.
I would as lief the shallow brook
    Had taught its fickle kiss to me
As seek by speech or glance the ways
    That I would fashion for thy praise.

I'll praise thee by remembering—
    Songs will I make thee from the sighs
Of mine own heart, and as I sing,
    The gentle river winds will rise,
As when, one day, their touch made rare
    Aeolian music through thy hair.

I'll praise thee by forgetfulness—
    I will forget the light of morn
Was ever fair, it is so less
    Fair than thine eyes; so, yet borne
Into one long, sweet dream of thee,
    Past and to come shall all dreams be.

THE DEAD GUN MAKER

Dead! and the belching thunder
    Of the guns on sea and shore,
Though they rive the world asunder,
    Can break on his ears no more.

Forth from his hands he sent them,
    Wherever men met as foes;
And, wherever strong hands unbent them,
    The cry of the wounded rose.

The groans of the maimed and dying,
    The moans of the ebbing heart,
On the fields of the dead, low lying,
    Were praise of his master art.

Wherever the ocean's billows
    The ships of the fleet have sped,
Deep over the coral pillows,
    Where the wild seas keep their dead;

Wherever, in rush or rally,
    Man clashed in the strife with man,
In Paardeberg's war-strewn valley,
    Or the red heights of Sedan,

Death and blood and disaster
    Spoke his great name in dread;
And now, in his shroud, the master
    That fashioned the guns lies dead.

BLOW, BUGLES, BLOW

Blow, bugles, blow, soft and sweet and low,
Sing a good-night song for them who bravely faced
    the foe;
        Sing a song of truce to pain,
        Where they sleep nor wake again,
        'Neath the sunshine or the rain—
Blow, bugles, blow.

Wave, banners, wave, above each hero's grave,
Fold them, O thou stainless flag that they died to
    save;
        All thy stars with glory bright,
        Bore they on through Treason's night,
        Through the darkness to the light—
Wave, banners, wave.

Fall, blossoms, fall, over one and all,
They who heard their country's cry and answered to
    the call;
        'Mid the shock of shot and shell,
        Where they bled and where they fell,
        They who fought so long and well—
Fall, blossoms, fall.

Sigh, breezes, sigh, so gently wandering by,
Bend above them tenderly, blue of summer sky;
      All their weary marches done,
      All their battles fought and won,
      Friend and lover, sire and son—
Sigh, breezes, sigh.

SICILY

Bride of the Sea and mistress of the Sun,
Ravished and wronged but ever loved the best—
Oh, weep for Sicily that lies undone,
Her children dead upon her withered breast.
Oh, weep for her whose beauty Homer sang,
Whose bosom knew a thousand lovers' tears,
Whose smile to gain, the world with battle rang,
And tides ran red through thrice a thousand years.

Of every sail the morning winds saw rise,
Of every spear and sword that served a King,
She was the best beloved, the fairest prize,
She that is now this broken, blackened thing.
Where crossed the trails she sat with luring lips,
Her breath like lemon bloom when day is sped,
The wanton plaything of the wandering ships.
Oh, weep for Sicily that now lies dead.

They who long wooed her in the storied past,
Her lovers all, what would they say if now
They could but see how prone she lies at last,
Beaten and scarred with black and bloody brow?
What would the old Phœnician say to this,
That was the dream to which with life he clung?
Vandal and Goth that died upon her kiss,
And they who loved her when the world was young?

Her sun has set as e'en the proudest must,
But she has stood 'gainst wrath of sea and fire
Till Rome and Carthage humbled were in dust,
And time had blasted Nineveh and Tyre.
They that she warmed within her sunny heart,
Whose star and crescent and whose cross she wore,
They, too, are dead and come not thus to part
With Sicily, whose beauty is no more.

TOLSTOI

[*Died, 1910*]

This is the thing, above all others,
The dead man did for us, my brothers—
He gathered the flags of a warring world,
 (All the banners beneath the sun)
With garlands of love their folds he furled,
 And bound them together every one.

'Tis not today, or perhaps tomorrow,
That joy shall come at the end of sorrow,
When sea and mountain, river and plain
 The sons of mothers no more divide.
But the time shall come when, in sun or rain,
 They will stand as brothers, side by side.

Hate shall fail, and the senseless clatter
Of spur and saber no more will matter;
Never again will the bugles call.
 (Lean shall the red-beaked vulture die)
Slav and Saxon, Teuton and Gaul,
 At night aweary in truce shall lie.

Yea, they shall sleep, the roar and rattle
Echoing from the last mad battle;
But they shall waken at break of morn,
    (The ramparts fallen, the battle done)
The wild bird's song in the springing corn,
    And the banners folded every one.

Then in the peace of golden weather,
Arm in arm, they will trudge together,
The bloodstains washed from love-clasped hands;
    (Goth and Mongol, Latin and Hun)
The world one nation of all men's lands,
    The fortress crumbled, the trenches won.

This is the thing, above all others,
The dead man did for us, my brothers—
For you and me and for men unborn.
    (Lyof, the Slav, who died today,)
Lyof, the Slav, whose feet have worn
    The man-made lines of the earth away.

SUNSET

Sunset, and the night comes on,
    The shouts, the clamors cease;
Upon the day's fierce Marathon
    Soft falls the hush of peace.

Light thou thy lamp that we may go
    Forth, and with silent tread,
Search for the fallen, lying low,
    The wounded and the dead.

The dead that we find lying there,
    They will not hear us call;
But we can ask, with many a prayer,
    Christ's pity on them all.

Fill thou thy gourd and we will roam
    Across the foughten fields,
And gently bear the wounded home
    Upon their broken shields.

We'll find them in the dew-red grass
    Where they lie bruised and spent;
Nor shall we linger as we pass
    The victor's boisterous tent.

We shall not wait to join his song,
    Nor sip his wassail free,
But press to where the conquered throng
    And where the vanquished be.

While high the victor's pæans roll,
    We'll seek with hurrying feet
The wavering heart, the faltering soul,
    That cower in defeat.

Sunset, and the night comes on,
    The stars gleam overhead.
Come, let us seek through Marathon,
    The wounded and the dead.

THE OLD REGIMENT

Long ago, on a summer's day,
Over the hills they marched away,
Kinfolk, friends and the boys we knew
In childhood's blossoms and fields of dew,
Changed in that hour to full-grown men
When the song of the bugle rang down the glen
With its wild appeal and its throb and thrall,
And they answered "Yea" to their country's call.

Then in the furrow the plowshare slept,
O'er wheel and anvil a silence crept;
All night long through the village street
Thundered the rhythm of marching feet,
With clash of steel and the saber's clang
And the gray commander's stern harangue,
Till morning broke, and they marched away,
Long ago, on a summer's day.

We watched them go with their guns agleam,
Down past the mill and the winding stream,
Across the meadows with clover deep,
By the old stone wall where the roses creep.
We watched them go till they climbed the hill,
And faced about as the drums grew still,
And waved their caps to the vale below
With its breaking hearts that loved them so.

Save for the maimed and the shattered few
They come no more to the vale they knew
In the old, dear days of their childhood's dreams;
But far away, by the alien streams,
On scenes of struggles their still hearts sleep,
Lying unnamed in the trenches deep
Where the foe at Antietam stormed the lines,
And the blood-stained bayonets of Seven Pines.

They wake no more to the battle's noise,
Kinfolk, friends and the neighbors' boys;
But oft, when the star-light fills the glen,
In phantom marches they come again.
And over the walls where the roses creep,
And the dew-kissed meadows with clover deep,
I see them still as they marched away
Long ago, on a summer's day.

ALWAYS THE FLAG OF THE FREE

Who fears for the flag that freedom blessed,
    Though it wanders afar from home,
By the winds caressed, to the East or West,
    Wherever its sons may roam?
In the calm of peace or the storm of wars
    On land or the bounding sea,
With its silver stars and its crimson bars
    It is always the flag of the free.

Far from the cradle where Liberty reared
    Its brood of free-born men,
That banner fared and has onward dared
    Full many a league since then.
Like a strong young eagle, on wings elate,
    It has followed its destiny
From the Old Bay State to the Golden Gate—
    The fetterless flag of the free.

God speed the flag that has never quailed,
    Though it rode o'er the Spanish Main;
When by foes assailed that has never failed
    Humanity's need and pain!
It shall bless the slave whom its valor frees,
    And its glory shall 'round him be;
On its own loved breeze or the Orient seas
    It is always the flag of the free.

ROBERT BURNS

"There was a lad was born in Kyle,"
    In Kyle among the hills of heather,
And 'tis tonight we'll sit awhile
    The songs he made to sing together;
Full many a stave that well we ken,
    The lilts beloved beyond all others,
The which that lifted lowly men
    As high as kings and made them brothers.

With his dear ghost we'll linger long
    Beside the hearthstone's glowing embers,
To dream of Robin and his song,
    The songs that all the world remembers.
We'll wander o'er the bonnie braes,
    With warlocks and the dancing fairy,
And linger by the winding ways
    Of Doon, to think of Highland Mary.

Dust are the heroes of the sword,
    Forgotten are the wars of Flanders,
With all the suns and rains that poured
    On slaughtered hosts and dead commanders.
What names they won who now will care?
    Time's mists enfold them and their story,
While from the hallowed fields of Ayr,
    One plowman stands in deathless glory.

THE NEW STAR ON THE FLAG

[*Oklahoma*]

Signal the fleets at sea,
    Shout to the forts ashore,
Round the world where the flag's unfurled,
    Let the deep-mouthed cannon roar.
On the singing winds of morn,
    Kissed by the drenching dew,
Old Glory waves, and a new star's born
    To gleam on its fields of blue.

Blow, O bugles, blow
    To echoing peak and crag,
And trumpets ring with a song to sing
    For the new star on the flag.
Another star is agleam,
    In the fadeless azure hung,
'Mid stripes of crimson and white that stream
    Wherever the flag is flung.

Tonight when o'er the deep
　　The path of the stars is spread,
Ghostly and pale again will sail
　　The ships of our mighty dead.
And John Paul Jones will cross the bar,
　　As oft in the deathless past,
And hoist the flag with its new-born star,
　　And nail it to the mast.

The word will pass, anon,
　　To the soldiers of the line,
To the camps ashore where met of yore
　　The bayonets at Brandywine;
From Monmouth's field 'twill speed
　　Onward to Marion's men;
Up where Mad Anthony sits his steed
　　In Stony Point's dim glen.

The new-born star will glow
　　On the spires of Fredericktown,
On the reeling lines at Seven Pines
　　And Mayre's Heights a-frown;
From Chicamauga's bloody tide,
　　And red Chantilly's fray,
'Twill follow on the dauntless ride
　　Where Sheridan won the day.

Blow, O bugles, blow,
    O'er hills and vales afar!
O'er peak and crag where flies the flag,
    There glows another star.
Deep where the shining cluster gleams,
    In the fadeless azure hung,
There's another star to light our dreams
    Wherever the flag is flung.

COSSACKS OF THE DON

The bugle rings, his steed he 'strides,
    The battle calls him on,
And forth to meet its shock he rides—
    The Cossack of the Don.
The fierce, red Tartar blood that flows
    Down from unconquered sires,
Wakes, with the joy his wild heart knows,
    When blaze war's flaming fires.

God help the foe that meets them when
    The Cossacks ride to war;
The strong, swift, bearded, fighting-men
    Whose friends the gray wolves are;
Who make their coverlets the snows
    When they lie down to sleep,
Who faster ride than wind that blows
    When they their saddles leap.

No man has seen the Cossack's sword
    Turn downward in the fight,
In vain have tides of battles poured
    Against them in their might;
The hoof-beats of their steeds are known,
    With all their wandering clan,
From bleak Siberian highways down
    To sun-kissed Astrakhan.

LITTLE BABE OF BETHLEHEM

When sang the stars together in the morning, long
    ago,
The Little Babe of Bethlehem slept in a manger low,
And wings of myriad angels swept the trembling
    mists of morn
When He who was the Prince of them in Bethlehem
    was born.

And yet, there was no diadem upon His brow to rest,
He had no pillow but the heart within His mother's
    breast;
His palace was a stable, bare of knight or paladin,
When Christ the Lord from Heaven came to free the
    world of sin.

His eyes were soft as summer skies, His brow as
    white as snow,
And round His head a halo shone like sunlight's
    golden glow,
And yet He lay an outcast, hid from Herod's cruel
    harm,
The Lamb of God that nestled upon His mother's
    arm.

O Little Babe of Bethlehem, I see Thee sleeping there;
I see Thine eyes like summer skies, Thy brow so
white and fair;
At Thy feet I see in wonder kneel the shepherds of
the fold,
I see the wise men's gifts of myrrh, and frankincense
and gold.

I see Thy mother Mary as in awe her hands caressed
Thy haloed head of glory as it lay upon her breast;
I hear her crooning to Thee in her mother love that
clings
To the soft hands that touch her lips as tenderly she
sings.

And, O dear Lord and Master, here is this heart of
mine,
Here is my homage and my love, and I am liege of
Thine.
Mine eyes behold Thy glory, at Thy feet my head
bends low,
As the shepherds bent when sang the stars of morn-
ing long ago.

THE FIRST SCHOOL DAY

The bells rang out their wild alarms
    One morning sweet and cool,
And then they scrubbed his wee brown arms
    And sent him off to school.
They robed the restless legs of him,
    They shod his bare, brown feet,
And sent him with his bright eyes dim,
    The vague, dread task to meet.

The squirrels on the old fence rail
    Chattered as he passed by,
And signaled with each bushy tail
    To bee and butterfly.
He wandered o'er the dimpled stream,
    That wept its tears of mists
To see him pass from lands o' dream
    With gyves upon his wrists.

Many a lingering look he turned
    Upon his fearsome road,
Hot was the heart that in him burned
    Beneath the cruel goad;
And when he turned and saw her there
    His mother at the gate—
He wrestled with his first despair,
    And railed his first at fate.

Well was it for his grand emprise
    That sped by mire and moat,
He could not see his mother's eyes
    Nor hear her sobbing throat;
He could but hear her cheery calls,
    And see her proud, high glance,
That bade him storm the foeman's walls
    With shield and lifted lance.

He left, at last, his native street,
    To brave strange fields and new,
The surging, alien crowds to meet
    Where friends were all too few;
He bravely passed with sturdy tread,
    Nor quailed at shout and din,
And lifted high his sunny head
    When closed his dungeon in.

O little boy, with heart care-free,
    O little bare, brown feet,
That wandered with the bird and bee
    On mornings cool and sweet,
Rough is the path you now must dare
    O'er valley, plain and hill;
But then, as now, while on you fare,
    May God be with you still.

THE GRAY DAY SHE DIED

The gray day she died, oh, 'tis long to recall,
    It is long to remember and long to forget;
The gray hill and glen and white mists over all,
    The dreary, dreary rain and the east winds wet.

It is long to remember, but I cannot forget;
    Though many a pathway my feet have wan-
        dered wide,
There never comes a gray day but I can see them yet,
    The hill and the valley and the place where she
        died.

They brought in the candles to light the solemn
        gloom,
    Candles for her feet and candles for her head;
We sat with broken voices in the silent, aching room,
    With the white mists weaving a shroud for the
        dead.

We saw the folded hands across the quiet breast,
    Her fingers entwined with her rosary of prayer,
And the east wind sobbing, it would not sink to rest,
    And the gray mists falling wet upon her hair.

It is long to remember, 'tis many a year since then,
   But I mind you coming in as though 'twere
      yesterday,
Saying, God was good to us, and well He loved us
      when
   He came on a gray day to take her away.

'Tis you that were knowing, 'tis you that were strong,
   When the white mists fell and the wet winds
      sighed—
Had a bird in the sun woke the lilt of his song
   Our hearts ne'er had borne it the gray day she
      died.

ALL SOULS' EVE

Clean shall the hearthstone be tonight,
    With glow of welcome spread
For them who come with footsteps light,
    The loved and wandering dead.

The dead who wander in the dark,
    Lonely and yet unshriven,
Till God on some glad day shall mark
    The sins of them forgiven.

For some there shall be glad release
    When dawns another morrow,
And some go still unblessed of peace
    Through many a day of sorrow.

But, one and all, tonight they'll come
    Through darkness and the cold,
Silent of step, unseen and dumb,
    To haunts beloved of old.

Then will the cheery embers glow,
    The waiting lamp be set,
That each dim silent guest may know
    He is remembered yet.

The feast is spread with kindly grace,
    On spotless linen fair,
And in each old, familiar place
    There waits the vacant chair.

O wandering dead tonight, who come
    Through darkness and the cold,
I sit not in the light of home
    To greet you as of old.

The waiting feast, all spread for you,
    No touch of mine shall know,
But you must still believe me true
    As in the long ago.

And when you look and find me not,
    You'll know, 'neath other skies,
I keep your vigil unforgot,
    And sit with sleepless eyes.

The wanderer by his roadside fire,
    His watch nor fails nor sleeps,
But, in his hungering heart's desire,
    The love of you he keeps.

And maybe so, with night still dim,
    'Ere light of morning streams,
Your wandering steps may come to him
    To cheer his lonely dreams.

And he may rise to feel you near,
    Rejoiced to know you came,
His soul athrill with joy to hear
    The whisper of his name.

CHRISTMAS

Some other time we will think of scars,
    Of the nails and the crown of thorn;
But today we will sing with the morning stars
    Of little King Jesus born.

Soft hands pressed to His mother's breast,
    Mary, the Jewish maid,
She croons the little King Jesus to rest
    Where His lowly bed is laid.

Some other time we will think of woe
    And the dust on His garment's hem,
And the weary road that He had to go
    From the stable of Bethlehem.

But now, as the shadow of night is spent,
    And morn with glad tidings thrills,
We will go the way that the Wise Men went,
    And the shepherds of the hills.

Today, when His baby finger tips
    Put hush on His mother's sighs,
There are smiles on little King Jesus' lips
    And laughter is in His eyes.

AMERICA

Mother, they came from the East and West,
    From the nether seas where the dim world dips,
And you bared to their need your tawny breast,
    Your young, sweet breasts to their eager lips.
They whom their own starved mothers flung
    On the ebb of wandering tides that call,
Till their alien arms were around you clung,
    And you gave them suckle and loved them all.

And side by side in their strength they grew,
    Saxon and Teuton and Celt and Dane,
Brood of the Briton where bleak winds blew,
    And warm skies bent o'er the brood of Spain.
From the nether seas, from the East and West,
    Till their blood was mingled in one red flow,
They that had slept on your tawny breast,
    O Mother of mine, in the Long Ago.

The blood of the world in one red flow,
　　Blue eyes that mated with raven hair,
And their sons were lusty to crush the foe,
　　And never were daughters as theirs so fair.
The forests fell where their rooftrees rose,
　　They dug the fields where the harvest smiles,
And their songs they echo from Arctic snows
　　To the palm-lined shores of the tropic isles.

In dreams of peace and in blood of wars,
　　In shock of battles that shook the world,
From summer rainbows and wintry stars,
　　They wove the banner no foe has furled.
Brood of the nations, they clasp your knee,
　　With steel they girt you from East to West,
And the touch of their hands is from sea to sea,
　　O Mother of mine with the tawny breast!

ST. JOHN, THE EVANGELIST

'Midst all the palm-crowned company
He seemeth always something more than they—
"Christ's own beloved John." Not Peter,
Even, the rock on whom he builded,
Nor Paul, the matchless silver-voiced,
Nor Thomas, with his hands upon his wounds,
Nor any of them all, down to this latest day,
Seem, my fair saint, so fair as thou,
"His own beloved John."

    Calm-eyed and sweet,
Almost as Christ to look upon, was he;
Almost the same soft, gentle way; with hair
That fell in waving locks his shoulders o'er,
And perfect brows, and perfect moulded mouth.
Too sad to smile, and yet in his fair face
Something more sweet and tender dwelt
Than that which lights the fondest mother's smile
Above her sleeping babe.

Beside Golgotha's cross
I often see that John divinely stand,
The last to hear his Master's last farewell
Through the drear agony of human pain.
I see the women clutching at his feet
Where stayed he when all other men had fled.
And then I love to watch him standing so,
To catch the glory of his dauntless eye,
And know that he who was the best beloved
Was faithful in the last and mightiest hour.

THE SONG OF THE FLAG

What song is the old flag singing,
    As it ripples upon the breeze,
Its voice to the far lands ringing,
    And its music upon the seas?
Oh, the light of its beauty's falling
    From the sweep of its own fair skies,
Through the gloom where the weak are calling,
    With hope in their lifted eyes.

Wherever its stars of glory,
    And its bars of crimson glow,
They will shine with the deathless story
    The world has thrilled to know.
And however the highways lengthen,
    Where the feet of freemen fare,
The song of the flag will strengthen
    The hearts that battle there.

And up where the white lands glisten
    In their jeweled robes of snow,
For the song of the flag they'll listen,
    With its music soft and low.
And down 'mid the palm trees sleeping,
    On shores of the sun-kissed main,
From the faith of their soul new-leaping,
    It will wake the glad refrain.

One land and one flag above it—
    From the ice-floes still and cold,
Borne on by the hearts that love it
    To the sunlit seas of gold;
With the gleam of its glory o'er them,
    To the restless winds unfurled,
Let them bear to the years before them
    Its challenge to all the world.

REQUIEM

When I have had my little day,
My chance at toil, my fling at play,
    And in the starry silence fall
    With broken staff against the wall,
May some one pass, God grant, that way,
And, as he bends above me, say:

"Good night, dear comrade, sleep you well,
Deep are the daisies where you fell;
    I fold your empty hands that shared
    Their little all with them that fared
Beside you in the rain and sun—
Good night, your little day is done."

Or, when my little hour has sped,
When night comes, and 'tis time for bed,
    The windows closed and locked the door,
    And I lie down to wake no more,
May some one at the break of day,
That comes to rouse me, wait to say:

"Farewell, dear comrade, mine no more;
A bird is singing at your door,
      And all the highways are athrong
      With steps you lightened with your song;
They come to call you from your bed—
Farewell, your little hour is sped."